Live Life Beyond The Laundry

7 Strategies to Shift Life From Chaos to Calm

Christy Tryhus

Live Life Beyond the Laundry
7 Strategies to Shift Life from Chaos to Calm

©Christy Tryhus
Simply Balanced Coaching and Training
809 Robinswood PL NE
Owatonna, MN 55060
www.SimplyBalancedCoaching.com

AKA-Publishing.com

Published in the United States of America

ISBN 978-1-936688-26-5
Trade Paperback
eBook ISBN 978-1-936688-30-2

Disclaimer

This book is designed to provide information and tools to help you move toward work/life balance. It is sold with the understanding that the publisher and author are not engaged in rendering psychiatric, legal, or other professional services. If psychiatric or other professional assistance is required, seek the services of a competent professional.

It is not the purpose of this manual to reprint all the information otherwise available to authors and/or publishers, but instead to complement, amplify and supplement other texts. You are urged to read all the available material, learn as much as possible about work/life balance and tailor the information to your individual needs.

Every effort has been made to make this manual as complete and as accurate as possible. Therefore, this text should be used only as a general guide. This manual contains information on work/life balance that is current only up to the printing date.

The purpose of this book is to educate. The author shall have neither liability nor responsibility to any person or entity with respect to any loss or damages caused, or alleged to have been caused, directly or indirectly, by the information contained in this book. If you do not wish to be bound by the above, you may return this book to the author/publisher for a full refund.

Table of Contents

v

Acknowledgements

The creation of this book has required the support of many people. I would first like to thank my husband Neil for encouraging me to follow my passion of helping people learn and grow to their fullest potential. Without his support I would not have been able to complete the journey of writing a book and creating a successful coaching and training business.

I would also like to thank my kids for their love, support and for allowing me to tell silly little stories about them in my book. Thank you, Amy, for all the extra time you dedicated to the success of this book. And finally, I would like to acknowledge the support of my parents and friends that provided their encouragement through this journey.

Thank you...I am grateful you are all a part of my life.

Foreword

I can clearly remember when I first met Christy. I was presenting at a coaching event and she came up afterward to introduce herself. I could immediately feel her energy, enthusiasm and passion for helping others. My instincts told me she was genuine, grounded and really good at coaching.

You're about to experience just how good she is at connecting people to personal insights that inspire growth. In the story that follows, Christy unfolds the universal truths women face juggling multiple roles. Her humor lightens some of the heavier truths. And her practical wisdom expands and opens up new possibilities. As she tells our collective story, you can't help but see reflections of yourself within it.

You'll quickly regain the clarity lost by the speed and busyness of life. And you'll be amazed at how easily the tools help you advance. The 7 Strategies blend introspection, common sense and real world application in simple action steps. You'll find important answers to many questions you've faced before, but not been able to answer.

The book you are holding will guide you to improve the quality of your life. Use the strategies to strengthen and grow. Work through the practices to increase your awareness and productivity. Let go of the excuses that have held you back and create the support you need to stay on track.

These ideas work. I've seen thousands of people successfully apply them over the past two decades. It is my hope that reading **Live Life Beyond the Laundry** will help you build the kind of life you want so you're truly happy, healthy and fulfilled.

Enjoy the journey!

Maryanne O'Brien
Live Dynamite, Founder, CEO

Introduction

When you're a little girl, no one tells you how much laundry you will have to do when you grow up. There should be more to life than laundry, more to life than sorting, folding, and searching for that missing sock. How can you move beyond the responsibilities and obligations that create chaos in your life and shift toward living a balanced life? The purpose of life is not making sure everyone has clean underwear.

So many women get caught up in their busy day-to-day schedules and responsibilities that they forget to enjoy life. Life was meant to be enjoyed, not just tolerated. **Live Life Beyond the Laundry** teaches strategies to successfully manage day-to-day schedules and responsibilities through a variety of activities and tools. The strategies are adaptable to take into account the special qualities of your family and life. Once you put these time-tested strategies and tools into action, you will lead a life of happiness, joy and fulfillment. You will achieve what most busy women only dream of: balance.

You may be asking: why **Live Life Beyond The Laundry**? That is how many women gauge their lives. I hear women say:

- "Just a minute. I need to throw in a load of laundry."
- "No, I can't go to a movie today. I need to catch up on the laundry."
- "Oh, I am so glad the weekend is here. I can catch up on the laundry."

An interesting fact: I did the math and I have completed roughly 7,500 loads of laundry over the last 25 years. That is a lot of laundry to do all while raising a husband, three kids, a cat and a dog. Do your math; you will be amazed.

Many women, and I assume you are one of them since you

purchased this book, don't begin living life or allowing themselves to enjoy life until the laundry is caught up. Based on this observation, I equate living life beyond the laundry to balancing your life. It's just my fun way of reminding myself of the importance of balancing life.

Living Life Beyond the Laundry = Balancing Life

Are you ready to begin living life to the fullest and enjoying life beyond the laundry? The decision is yours. If you answered a whole-hearted YES, read on.

Before you begin to create successful change in your life, you must understand one critical key. Successful change requires a clear vision of what you want to achieve. **Live Life Beyond the Laundry** will help you create the ideal vision of what you want your life to look like. Once you have created the vision, you will learn how to create action plans using the strategies and tools highlighted in each chapter. Finally, one last critical component: You will learn how to celebrate your success. That's your reward for doing the hard work.

So many of us plan and plan and forget to do. When you complete the activities in the following chapters and put them into action in your life, I guarantee you will increase your happiness, work/life balance and overall joy for life.

Let's look at it a different way: A carpenter would not get very far building a house if he or she didn't have a blueprint, organized daily plan, hammer and saw. This book is your blueprint, and each chapter will explain how to correctly use the tools and strategies in the work/life balance toolbox. Learn how to utilize the right tools at the right time to take life from chaos to calm. You are constructing your life the way you want it to be.

Create your best possible life by first following a blueprint (this book) and then using the correct tools (the 7 Strategies) to achieve the desired results. In **Live Life Beyond the Laundry,** each tool is designed to meet the unique needs of your family. Learn how to apply the tools to achieve your desired life. It's not enough to learn about them; you must put them into action. Why wait another day? Begin to **Live Life Beyond The Laundry** today. The key to success is using the tools on a daily basis. Daily action creates results.

You may be thinking, as most women do, "I am too busy to do any more. My life is crazy busy already." Reframe your thinking. You are too busy not to learn how to manage your day-to-day schedules and responsibilities better. Begin today; put the first strategy into action and notice the results. I am not expecting you to move a mountain. Making positive changes in life is all about taking baby steps. As I mentioned above, daily action creates results.

Below is an overview of the 7 Strategies to take life from chaos to calm. By the end of this book, you will have a complete understanding of each strategy and will fully understand how each tool in the work/life balance toolbox can benefit your life.

These strategies are ten years in the making. I have studied, honed and adapted the tools to create a high-quality work/life balance toolbox. This is my gift to you; I have done the research for you. Consider me your research assistant. I have created the tools for you to tackle the job; all you have to do is put them to work.

In the following pages, I have given you a brief description of each of the 7 Strategies you will learn to implement in your life. These will give you a taste of what each of the strategies entails.

Strategy #1: "Me" Time. It is important to take time for yourself each day. If you don't take care of yourself, you won't be able to take care of others to the best of your ability. "Me" Time recharges your battery and allows you to operate throughout your day fully charged. Strategy #1 focuses on tools to build "Me" Time into your daily routine. Learn how to put yourself at the top of your daily "to do" list.

Strategy #2: Ask for help. Busy women think they can do it all—all by themselves. Admit it, girls; you think that unless you do it yourself, it won't get done correctly. So you power through the day, accomplishing task after task, then collapse into bed at the end of the day. Well, ladies, if you help each other out, you will be more productive and have more time for "Me" Time, family time and, even better, less chaos. Strategy #2 focuses on tools to incorporate asking for help into your daily routine.

Strategy #3: NO is not a four-letter word. If the words, "Yes, I can help with that" or "Sure, I can make that work" are part of your daily vocabulary, this strategy will transform your life. Busy women tend to overcommit and spread themselves so thin they don't have time for their families, let alone themselves. Strategy #3 focuses on tools to help you learn to say YES when you really want to say YES and say NO when you don't want to do something. NO is a complete sentence!

Strategy #4: Balancing act. In essence, this strategy discusses time management that works. No matter how many things you can juggle or multi-task, there are still only 24 hours in a day. Time is the only commodity you cannot purchase more of, so you must use the minutes you have wisely. Strategy #4 focuses on tools for planning, dividing and conquering the day for success.

Strategy #5: Stop procrastinating NOW. There are many reasons why we procrastinate and, yes, ladies, we all procrastinate in some way, shape or form. Simply put, procrastination wastes time, decreases productivity and allows chaos to bloom. Learn about the different types of procrastination and how to build success tools to reduce its power over your life. Once you understand why you procrastinate, the tools will be easier to incorporate into daily life.

Strategy #6: Busy Mind Syndrome. Otherwise known as BMS, this is the tendency we have to let all the things we faced, done and undone, to clutter our brains. BMS makes it difficult to sleep and focus on your daily schedules and responsibilities. This strategy focuses on understanding the root cause of BMS and how to use the tools to reduce it. Some of the common causes are mommy guilt, over-committed schedule, unrealistic expectations, and the never-ending to-do list. Let's face it; who doesn't want a little less BMS in their lives?

Strategy #7: Don't Reinvent the Laundry Basket. Simply put, we all have tips, strategies and tools we use each day. Ladies, share the knowledge. Why reinvent the laundry basket? Many of the tools in Strategies #1 through #6 I learned from friends, family and co-workers. Yes, some of them I modified to meet the unique needs of my family; however, I learned them from others. So, if you have a tool or strategy that works, share it. This strategy is a compilation of miscellaneous tips and success stories I learned from friends, family and co-workers.

Working through this book is a process. You have a choice to work through one strategy or several at a time. You set the pace; this is your journey. It is not a book to read cover to cover. Work through the strategies at your pace. As you progress through the activities, you will know when you are ready to integrate a new strategy into your life.

Living Life Beyond the Laundry = Balancing Life

Vision without action is merely a dream. Action without vision just passes the time. Vision with action changes the world. ~Joel A. Barker

Chapter 1

Busy Bizzy

You need not feel guilty about not being able to keep your life perfectly balanced. Juggling everything is too difficult. All you really need to do is catch it before it hits the floor! ~Carol Bartz, CEO. Yahoo

Before we begin learning about the 7 Strategies to take your life from chaos to calm, I would like to share with you why I have developed passion for this topic. I have spent the last ten years researching, honing and incorporating these success strategies into my life.

My journey to **Live Life Beyond the Laundry** began back in 2002 when the stress and chaos in my life began to affect my health and the quality of my life. I knew things had to change and that it was up to me to make that happen. Thus, my journey, research and transformation began.

My family consists of my wonderful husband and three great kids. Oh, and I can't forget our dog and cat. I worked as a sales representative and corporate sales trainer for a successful organization. I was also part of a project team implementing a significant change in the company. The responsibilities became overwhelming, resulting in stress and chaos in my life. I tried to balance (unsuccessfully) my daily expectations and responsibilities at work and home.

The stress and chaos began to take a toll. When I finally headed for home at the end of the day, I still had at least 20 things left on my work to-do list. The result was that I took work home with me in the form of busy mind syndrome (BMS) every day. This created a grouchy, edgy mom and wife. This is not how I wanted to be, but I was not in control. Stress and chaos had taken over my life. I knew I had to make a change when I began suffering from short-term memory loss.

That was the day I began reading and researching about work/life balance and organizing my life. Did you know people can successfully enjoy work and home life? I began to implement and modify work/ life balance tools to meet the needs of my family. The tools worked, the short-term memory loss reversed itself, and I began to enjoy my evenings and weekends with the family.

This is how I live my life now. Every tool and strategy discussed in this book has been gradually implemented in my life. As a result of my hard work and consistent action, I have learned to shift my life from chaos to calm. Is my life calm and serene every day? NO. Is that okay? YES. See, NO is a complete sentence.

What I have learned is how to notice the signs and signals when my life is getting too chaotic and stressful. That is when a clear understanding of the 7 Strategies and tools in this book becomes extremely important. I figure out what is creating the chaos and build a strategy to shift back to calm.

I did not accomplish this overnight. It is a journey that takes daily action. As mentioned above, I occasionally slip, but I recognize the signs of stress and chaos much faster now and begin moving forward again with the use of the 7 Strategies. I sometimes refer to these as my work/life balance toolbox.

If I can make these changes, anyone can. I spent hours reading and researching this topic. You have a leg up on me; I have completed the research for you! Now it is your turn to do a little work.

First, you must understand the process and importance of making positive change in your life. During this transformation/journey, you will gain an understanding of where you currently are in your life and then identify your challenges and obstacles. Learn what is getting in your way of living life to the fullest. Then create powerful action items and goals to move yourself forward, setting milestones during the journey to celebrate your success.

Celebrating your success keeps you moving forward. Let's face it; we all like to be rewarded for our hard work. You can achieve a happy, fulfilling life by incorporating the "**Live Life Beyond the Laundry**" strategies into your life. It works. I am living proof.

Don't let excuses get in your way of happiness. I often ask people,

"How are you today"? The answer 80% of the time is "so busy." I then take it one step further and ask, "What are you so busy with"? Most people can't answer that question. They have to think about it. We have turned into a "busy" society. Many of us equate busyness to productivity. This is so far from the truth. Busy does not equal productive. It makes you feel like you are productive but, at the end of the day, what have you really accomplished?

So what are we so busy doing?

• Laundry
• Email
• Social media
• Solving problems and issues at work and home
• Going to meetings
• Playing taxi driver to kids
• Picking up after the family
• Watching TV
• Consuming time with mommy guilt
• Thinking about all the things we should have gotten done
• And the list goes on and on, tumbling in the dryer

Many of the items listed above include technology. Wasn't technology meant to make our lives more efficient and productive? In many aspects, it has. However, it has also become a huge time drain. Don't get me wrong; social media and more online shopping can be fun and both serve a purpose. Who doesn't love catching up with your friends, finding good shopping deals, all while snuggling up on your sofa under a warm, fuzzy blanket and enjoying a great cup of coffee? Sounds fantastic but, before you know it, two hours have passed and you are suddenly aware of how much you could and should have gotten done in those two hours. Thus begins the chaos.

Let's take a different perspective to deepen our understanding of the overall effect technology has placed on our daily lives. Many of us were not born in the 1950s, but did you know that, in the 1950s, futurists predicted that by the year 2000 most people would only work 20 to 30 hours per week? This prediction was based on the evolution of machines and technology and how they would aid us both at work and at home. The futurists predicted people would have so much leisure time they would not know how to keep themselves busy. Boy, they really blew that one, didn't they?

We all know this wealth of free time is far from the truth. Little did the futurists know that the advances in machines and technology would speed life up. We have seen our leisure time shrink and our work week increase to over 40 hours per week, just to keep up with our over-flowing inboxes and flood of electronic communication. Computers and high-speed printers can create 70 letters in just minutes, a task that used to take a secretary a couple of days to complete. Technology did not free us as once predicted; it forced us to work at its speed.

It's time to slow down to move faster. Think about it. This is something I frequently tell myself when I start feeling a bit stressed or chaotic. This small statement, slow down to move faster, works every time.

Remember, no one else can do this for you. The choice is yours. No action, no reward. I have refined the strategies and tools over time to create the best tools for busy women. I am sharing the results of my success. The key is that you cannot just read about the tools; you must put them into action. Begin now so you can start to **Live Life Beyond the Laundry** today.

Experience how great life can be through the eyes of Elizabeth Tisdale. Elizabeth recently made changes in her life and she would like to share a glimpse of her crazy, busy life with you. When I first met Elizabeth, she lived a very stressful, busy life consumed with guilt, worry and chaos. She was not really enjoying her kids, job or significant other. She wanted to make some changes and live life to the fullest. She realized she had hit a point of extreme chaos and was completely overwhelmed. She needed to make some changes, and so began Elizabeth's journey of transformation. Let's meet Elizabeth.

Meet Elizabeth

I would like to take a few minutes to introduce myself. My name is Bizzy. Actually, my name is Elizabeth, but my friends and family call me Bizzy because it is the one word that describes my life. At first, I was annoyed by this nickname; however, I have now come to realize it fits. So I have just accepted the fate and deal with it.

To set the scene for my life, let's fill in the details. I am married with three kids, one dog, one cat, and four goldfish. We live in a comfortable home, big enough for the five of us. We have a great yard, neighborhood and town. Sounds perfect. That is the postcard version we sell every year in our Christmas card.

Let's rephrase and do a reality check. To set the scene for my life, let's fill in the (non-Christmas card) details. I am the mother of three kids, four if you count my husband, and I can't seem to quite catch up with things in life. Oh, and my kids actually have a cat, a dog and four goldfish as well, and we all know what that means—more responsibility for mom, yay!

We have a comfortable home scattered with toys and stacks of paper. I figure if the paper sits there long enough, it will become garbage. We have a great yard, the one chore my husband actually assumes responsibility for. We have great neighbors, not that I am actually sure because I don't have any time to spend with them. My husband assures me they are awesome!

I never intended to have my life become this busy; it just happened. One day I woke up wishing I had 35 hours each day instead of 24. If I had 35 hours each day I would have time for my kids, my husband and myself. See, I just need more time, and then everything would be perfect. However, I always have this nagging feeling that I am a little behind or forgetting something.

The other feeling I have from time to time is mommy guilt. I always have good intentions to spend more time with my kids but laundry, cleaning the kitchen, work emails and errands take longer than I plan, thus cutting into my time with the kids. They seem to be getting used to it, but I know in my heart it is wrong. One time I tried to play Monopoly while checking my emails. I thought it was working fine; however, my kids did not agree. Oh, the memories I create!

I attempt to balance work and family with a really long—and I mean really long to-do list. But I still have a nagging, stressful feeling running through me. It just does not go away. I am crazy busy.

Whenever I check one item off the infamous to-do list, three more items magically appear. My ultimate goal is to conquer the day in an orderly fashion. This does not always happen; quite often the day results in some form of chaos or drama. I need to make some changes in my life before it runs me over completely.

If you think this story sounds familiar, or if you gave a little giggle inside as you read about Bizzy, you might just see a little of Bizzy in yourself. What does Bizzy do each day? Well, let's just take a look at her typical morning and you will get the point.

A Typical Bizzy Day

5:45: Ugh, the alarm is going off already. (I am so tired… what day is it, anyway? Is it Thursday? No, it's Tuesday.)

5:49: Roll out of bed and take the dog outside. (No matter

how cold or rainy. Oh, yay, snow.)

5:58: Feed and water the dog. (I need to get one of those auto dispensers. I have to put that on my to-do list.)

6:05: Shower time. (Have to beat my teenager to the shower before she uses all the hot water. I need to buy one of those shower timers. That will teach her to take a 26-minute shower! Put that on my to-do list.)

6:12: Felt good to take a shower. Coffee time… (I love my coffee.)

6:45: Wake up the kids. Let the chaos begin! (Seriously, did I just think that about my kids?)

6:50: Make the kids breakfast. (Wish I could just throw some dry cereal on the plate. That would be just as easy as feeding the dog. Maybe they make automatic cereal feeders for kids.)

6:55: Round up backpacks, coats, shoes. (Why is this my job???)

7:05: Tell the kids to get dressed for school. (You would think they could figure that out. They do it every day.)

7:06: Run back to my room to get ready for work.

7:08: Ugh. Tell kids to get dressed again. (Seriously?)

7:09: Run back to my room to finish getting ready for work.

7:10: "Come on, kids… bathroom duty time, hair, teeth, deodorant, get it done." (Want your friends to say you stink and have ugly hair? This is really not my problem; it's yours.)

7:15: Did you do your bathroom duty, kids? Hair, teeth, deodorant…get it done or you are going to bed early tonight.

7:20: Finish getting ready. The bus will be here in four minutes.

7:21: Mom, I need you to sign my permission slip for the field trip. (Seriously, could she not have asked me this last night?)

7:22: Mom, I need $10 for a band t-shirt. It's due today. (Again, why did she not ask me last night?)

7:23: Come on! You're going to miss the bus. (Great, now I had to yell at them as they were leaving for school.)

7:24: Yes! The kids are at the bus stop.

7:28: Put the breakfast dishes in the dishwasher.

7:30: Take dog outside. (I feel so bad I yelled at the kids on their way out the door.)

7:40: On the road to work—finally!

7:55: And the work day has begun. (Why do I feel so stressed today? I really wish I had not yelled at the kids on their way out the door.)

8:00: Call from the school: "Mom, I forgot my tennis shoes for gym. Can you bring them? (Seriously?) "Sure, honey, I will bring them right away."

8:20: Back to work.

9:00: Meeting.

10:00: Meeting.

11:00: Catch up on email.

12:00: Lunch hour. (Oh, I mean errand hour—grocery store, bank, post office.)

You get the picture. And the chaos and mommy guilt continue throughout the day. Look at all the chaos and stress created in just a mere 2 hours and 15 minutes before Bizzy even went to work. What a way to start the day! Back to Bizzy.

Whew, I made it through the work day. It would have gone a little better if I had not yelled at the kids as they left this morning. I have to hurry and get the kids picked up from after-school care; it closes in 15 minutes. I will not be that mom who is late picking up her kids.

I will be there in eight minutes and will have seven minutes to spare, so I am not one of those moms. Yay, me! Wow! Traffic is really backed up. OH?!/% A TRAIN! I did not build that into my timing. So I may be one of those moms running through the door of after-school care apologizing and making up excuses why I am late. Good thing I can blame it on the train.

Good, that was a fast train. I have made it to after-school care with one minute to spare…at least according to my clock. Hi, kids. I am so sorry I yelled at you this morning.

Who has homework? Hope it's not too much. We have piano and football practice tonight. Oh, I forgot about supper. I am so hungry. I guess I forgot about lunch as well. Kids, what do you want from Zippy Burger tonight? Sorry, but we need to eat in the car again. (Oh, how I hate Zippy Burger).

It is so nice that football and piano overlap. I have 15 minutes to read my magazine in the car. Time to pick up the kids and rush home to finish homework. Kids, shower time, bedtime and don't forget to brush your teeth. Oh, they are finally in bed. I am so tired. I need to start a load of laundry or there will be someone without underwear in the morning. Who needs that drama?

Flop! Finally I can go to bed. I wonder what I forgot to do. That big project at work is not going so well. Tomorrow I am not going to yell at the kids on their way out the door. I wonder if someone fed the dog. I really need to go to sleep. I am tired. How are we going to make it to football, conferences and dance all at the same time tomorrow? I really need some sleep.

BBBBBBZZZZZZZ! (*%&#) That alarm gets earlier every morning. Oh, guess I was wrong. It is 5:45. I really need to get up a little earlier and go for a walk in the morning. Whatever, I need the sleep.

I am so tired of being this busy. I want to read a book or get a pedicure or watch a movie I like. But my kids and work must come first. It's okay that I am not part of my daily to-do list. I can just wish I had the time for a pedicure or to read a good book. My friend Ann always finds time to read books. I wonder how she does that. She must ignore her kids, and I bet her house is a mess.

When I first met Bizzy, her life was filled with chaos, worry, mommy guilt and excuses. She needed a change. She incorporated the strategies you will learn about in the next eight chapters into her daily routine, and her life has changed drastically. At the conclusion of the book, she will share with you how she lives her life now. You will be amazed by the change. The tools and strategies work if you incorporate them into your daily life. Daily action creates results.

So let's begin.

Before we dig into the 7 Strategies, it is important to briefly discuss the process we go through when making changes in our lives. The topic of change is discussed in Chapter 2. In Chapter 3 we will discuss making excuses. Admit it, ladies, we all make them. Excuses are the source of obstacles and barriers that prevent us from creating successful change. After learning about the change process and excuses, we will dive into the strategies. Enjoy your journey!

Living Life Beyond the Laundry = Balancing Life

"The essential question is not how busy are you?
But what are your busy at?" ~*Oprah Winfrey*

Chapter 2

Understanding Change

"To change one's life: Start immediately, Do it flamboyantly, no exceptions." ~William Jones, Philosopher

Before we begin learning and applying the 7 Strategies to shift life from chaos to calm, it is important to understand the different stages of change. The change created by applying the strategies and tools in **Live Life Beyond the Laundry** is more than a New Year's resolution. If done correctly, it's a sustainable lifestyle change!

Many of the coaching clients I work with want change to happen overnight. I'm sorry to tell you it doesn't happen that fast. Successful, positive change takes time and work. You really have to want the end result of the change to make the change happen. Consistent daily action sustained over a period of time creates results. During the change process, you are basically reprogramming your brain.

Scientists believe that 90 percent of our day-to-day activities are spent in routine. This is a good thing. This means we just know how to brush our teeth, turn on the shower, make a bowl of cereal or even read a book. You have practiced these activities with such consistency and frequency that you have created pathways in your brain to repeat the sequences without even thinking about them.

This is also a bad thing. You have developed unhealthy, destructive routines as well—for example, creating unrealistic expectations, telling yourself you are so busy, multi-tasking, and telling yourself you don't have the time.

My coaching clients who have successfully implemented even some of the tools and strategies in this book reap benefits for a lifetime. The strategies work. I challenge you to make a few small changes. The strategies in this book are something you will gradually implement into your life. If you try to tackle all 7 Strategies, you will become overwhelmed and will not sustain the lifestyle changes. So pick three areas you need the most work on and start there.

According to James Prochaska and a team of scientists from the University of Rhode Island, there are five stages to the change process. These scientists developed a model for change called the Transtheoretical Model. To successfully achieve your dreams and goals, you will progress through each of the following stages.

1. **Pre-contemplation** (Not Ready)—People don't even know they need or want to change.
2. **Contemplation** (Getting Ready)—People begin to recognize they need to change a behavior and start to look at the pros and cons. They say, "Someday I will do that."
3. **Preparation** (Ready)—People intend to take action soon and may begin taking small steps toward making changes.
4. **Action** (Making progress)—People take specific actions and make modifications.
5. **Maintenance** (Keep going and celebrate success)— People are able to sustain the actions and modifications for a period of time.

By understanding the five stages of change, you will increase your probability of success to **Live Life Beyond the Laundry**. Since you have purchased this book, you are likely somewhere between the stages of contemplation and preparation.

You can work through the book from Strategy #1 to Strategy #7, or you can identify the areas creating the biggest challenges in your life and start there. Either will be effective, since all 7 Strategies are important to your ability to **Live Life Beyond the Laundry**. If you are reading this book with an e-reader, purchase a cute journal to complete the activities. The following activity will help you determine the starting point for your journey of change and success.

Where Are You Now in Your Continuum?

The purpose of this activity is to identify which of the 7 Strategies you excel at and which need some improvement. It is crucial to get an understanding of what is creating the chaos and frustration in your life. This activity will guide you through a self-analysis to determine where to begin to shift life from chaos to calm.

Step 1: Rate yourself from 1 (clueless) to 10 (kickin' butt) for each of the 7 Strategies. When you rank yourself, be brutally honest because, if you are not, the only person you hurt is you. It is your starting point. (I have provided a short explanation of each strategy below to create understanding as you rank yourself.)

(Clueless) 1   2   3   4   5   6   7   8   9   10 (Kickin' Butt)

___ Strategy #1: "Me" Time—Time spent each day doing something you enjoy. "Me" Time recharges your battery and allows you to operate throughout your day fully charged.

___ Strategy #2: Ask for help—As busy women, we think we can do it all, and all by ourselves. We power through the day, task after task, then collapse into bed at the end of the day. Learn to incorporate asking for help into your daily routine without feeling guilty about it.

___ Strategy #3: NO is not a four-letter word—If the words, "Yes, I can help with that" or "Sure, I can make that work" are part of your daily vocabulary, this strategy will transform your life. As busy women, we tend to over-commit and spread ourselves so thin we don't have time for our families, let alone ourselves.

___ Strategy #4: Balancing act—In essence, this strategy discusses effective time management. It is a commonly known fact that there are only 24 hours in a day; once you use those hours, they are gone. Strategy #4 focuses on tools for planning, dividing and conquering the day for success.

___ Strategy #5: Stop procrastinating NOW—We all procrastinate to some degree or another. Procrastination wastes time, decreases productivity and causes chaos. How much time do you spend procrastinating?

___ Strategy #6: Busy Mind Syndrome—Are you always thinking about too many things? This is Busy Mind Syndrome, otherwise known as BMS, which makes it difficult to sleep and to focus on your daily schedules and responsibilities.

___ Strategy #7: Don't reinvent the laundry basket—Everyone has tips, strategies and tools to make the day run smoother. Do you ask friends and family what works for them? Ask; you might be amazed at what you learn.

Step 2: Put a star next to the two highest scores. Now, use the space below to make a list of everything you do well in these areas of your life. It is important to give yourself credit for what you already do well. Take a moment and reread this list. Celebrate and congratulate yourself on every single one of the things you already do to control the chaos in your life. If your list is short, that's okay. If your list is empty, that's okay. Taking the steps you have taken so far in this process is a giant leap in the right direction. Continue these activities as you begin to work on the areas you have identified that need a little work.

Step 3: Circle the two lowest scores. These are the areas of focus as you begin to work through the book. As mentioned above, you may choose to begin to work on these strategies first or begin working through the book from Strategy 1.

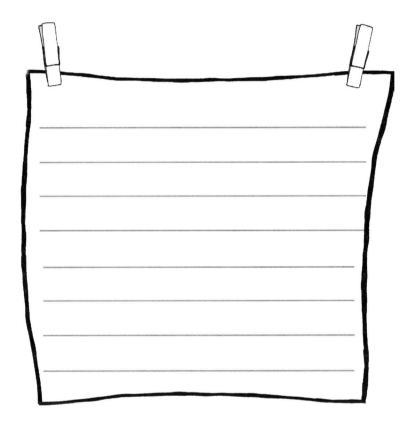

Where Do you Want to Be?

The purpose of this activity is to create a vision of what you want your future to look like. When you create a clear, concise vision of what you want, it greatly increases the probability it will happen.

Step 1: Spend time giving thought to what you want to have. Dream big. The sky's the limit. Create your ideal life. What do you want the following items in your life to look like? Write down your answers in the space provided.

- Fun: happiness, hobbies
- Relationship: current or future life partner
- Career: job satisfaction, career path
- Family: children, parents, relatives
- Social: friends, sport, activities
- Health: exercise, diet, "Me" Time
- Financial: savings, investments
- Spirituality: faith

Step 2: Imagine you have already reached the above dreams and goals. What does it feel like right now to have that in your life? Write it down. Do you feel happy, excited, grateful and fulfilled?

Step 3: Now, believe you already have this life. Live as if you have created success. Fake it until you make it. In time, it will be your new reality. This creates the emotional connection to truly reach your dreams.

Step 4: Take it one step further and create a vision board. Find pictures in magazines or on the internet that represent your vision of how life will be when you reach your dreams. These are pictures that inspire you. Glue the pictures to a large sheet of paper and place your vision board where you will see it daily. I have mine on my desk. You don't need to study it every day. Just by glancing at it occasionally, you will remain inspired to move forward to reach your dreams. If you enjoy technology, you can also create an electronic vision board that sequences through when you log on to your computer each morning. Here is a picture of my first vision board.

Success Story:

A coaching client of mine has been using a vision board for a couple of years. She shared with me that she created one several months back in a class. She tucked it away in the class material and forgot to put it in a location where she would see it. One of the items she placed on the vision board was a picture of Disney World. Her dream was to take her daughter to Disney World. She knew it was a stretch; however, she placed it on her vision board anyway. She just returned from her trip to Disney World with her daughter. She had forgotten she had placed it on her vision board. Just a few months back, it was only a dream and it magically materialized just by creating the vision.

Fun Story:

A good friend of mine created a travel vision board. She cut out pictures of every place she dreams of traveling to sometime in the future. She then created a vision board with the pictures. As she travels to her dream locations, she glues a picture she took during her travels and places it over the cut-out picture of that location on her vision board. This is the power of turning dreams into reality.

Living Life Beyond the Laundry = Balancing Life

You can't make your dream happen if you don't have a dream! ~Walt Disney

Chapter 3

Understanding Excuses

No one ever excused his way to success. ~Dave Del Dotto

In the previous chapter we developed a deeper understanding of the change process. Understanding how to change is critical to your ability to **Live Life Beyond the Laundry**. Why is it so hard to change sometimes? The answer: Excuses. What is the origin of those excuses? You! Yes, you create the excuses that slow you down or even stop progress toward achieving success, goals and sometimes even happiness. Excuses contribute to stress, chaos and negative self-talk.

Think of the change process as taking a hike down a mountain path. You are excited as you begin your hike because of the green vegetation, beautiful wildflowers and wildlife you encounter along the way. As you continue on the journey, the path narrows and becomes rocky and steep. You want to continue because the hike has been great so far. However, it is getting difficult. The naturalist told you there is a beautiful waterfall that cascades into an emerald lake at the end of the hike. She assures you it is worth the tough journey. You really want to see that waterfall and would be so proud of the pictures you could take. What an accomplishment! However, you are not sure you want to continue because it is really difficult, it will take so much time, and you're tired. What should you do? The choice is yours.

This is a common dilemma of many of my coaching clients. They develop this fantastic goal and are excited about their journey, but then they get stuck. They begin to think it's too hard or they don't have the time to do the work required to be successful. They have just encountered an obstacle or a challenge.

When you reach this point in your journey, you have a choice: To build a strategy to move forward or create an excuse and quit. The choice is yours. We all make excuses in our lives; however, successful people move beyond the excuses and take themselves to the next level. They reach fulfillment, happiness and joy in their lives. They begin to **Live Life Beyond the Laundry**.

In my years as a coach, trainer and educator, I have heard many excuses why people cannot reach their goals and dreams. In general, we all have the same excuses. They fall into the following categories:

1. I don't have enough time. I am too busy.
2. I will do it when my kids grow up.
3. It will be too difficult.
4. I am afraid.
5. I don't know if I am willing to take that risk.
6. What would my parents think?
7. I cannot afford it.
8. I can't do that by myself and no one will help me.
9. I'm too old or not old enough.
10. I don't have the energy. I'm too tired.

These are all great reasons—I mean excuses—and it's up to you to push through them. Successful people never quit; they stumble along the way and learn lessons when they trip. But they pick themselves up and continue on.

Many of my coaching clients experience setbacks, challenges and obstacles. When this happens, I say, "You have taken twenty steps forward over the past couple of months and you just took four steps back. So what? Are you going to let those steps back get in the way of your success? Look at how far you have come. The choice is yours, though. We can build a strategy to move you forward again or you can slip a few more steps back; it's your choice."

Guess what the answer always is? Build a strategy to move forward again.

So what should you do to eliminate excuses? We all have excuses; however, some people know how to push through them. You can, too. The following are tools to help you push through excuses when obstacles and challenges are blocking the path to your goal.

- Be positive: We all create excuses because we don't feel like doing something. We create a negative image in our head of how hard or time-consuming something might be. Instead, see the fun in something and maintain a positive attitude. Using this approach, you will beat the excuse.
- Build a strategy: This book is filled with tools and techniques to help you beat excuses. Basically, you are finding a solution. Every problem has a solution, so find it and put it into action.
- Take responsibility: It's easier to blame someone or something else than it is to take responsibility. If you own up to the problem, it is easier to find a solution to move forward.
- Set a goal: Create a clear and concise goal and visualize it. When you see yourself achieving your goal, you will become motivated to move forward.
- Find an accountability partner: This can be a friend, co-worker, or life coach. For example, you are more likely to get out of bed in the morning for 5:45 a.m. boot camp class if you are meeting your friend there.

Use these tools to move beyond the excuses, achieve your goals and dreams, and lead a happy fulfilling life.

> *Pessimism is an excuse for not trying and a guarantee*
> *to a personal failure. ~Bill Clinton*

Chapter 4

The Power of a Positive Attitude

Happiness is an attitude. We either make ourselves miserable, or happy and strong. The amount of work is the same. ~Francesca Reigler

The daily habit of a positive attitude is a key ingredient to help you **Live Life Beyond the Laundry**. A positive attitude creates positive emotions, such as happiness, joy and fulfillment. Everyone is capable of creating a life of happiness, joy, and fulfillment. A positive attitude makes the journey easier and greatly increases your probability of success. Think about it this way: attitudes are contagious. Is yours worth catching?

You may think your life is busy, crazy, and chaotic, so how can you even think about having a positive attitude? You're thinking to yourself, "I simply have an attitude; that's okay." You now have a starting point for the transformation to **Live Life Beyond the Laundry**.

For the last ten years, interest in positive psychology has become a growing trend. Research in this field demonstrates that positive emotions strengthen your ability to change your perceptions so you can see all that is possible in your life. More and more people are searching for information on how they can achieve their full potential and become more fulfilled. According to Dr. Timothy J. Sharp, author of *100 Ways to Happiness*, positive psychology is, at least in part, about taking a proactive approach to CREATING happiness, rather than just WAITING for it to happen.

When you change the way you think, you open the door to positive change. A positive attitude changes how your mind works. It's an essential step to successfully implementing **Live Life Beyond the Laundry** strategies. When you maintain a positive attitude, you are able to stay inspired and focused so you can make the necessary changes to live life to the fullest.

According to Maryanne O'Brien, founder of the *Live Dynamite Life Skills* program, living life with a positive attitude or positive emotions leads to higher levels of self-awareness and self-perception. When you feel positive, you tend to live mindfully. You stay tuned in to how you think and feel. This increased level of self-awareness allows you to notice when you slip into a downward spiral so you can pull yourself out of it. The study of positive psychology has proven there are enormous benefits to creating a positive mindset/attitude every day.

Maryanne states that positive emotions allow you to expand and unlock more of your potential. Optimism strengthens your ability to feel inspired, creative and receptive. This helps you see new opportunities, identify potential paths to achieve your goals, and take action. It gives you the ability to step back from challenges, generate solutions, and continue to experiment.

Living life with a positive attitude increases happiness and your ability to strive for increased work/life balance. During my **Live Life Beyond the Laundry** presentations, I always discuss the power of a positive attitude. Many people feel they already have a positive attitude and mindset. If you fall into that category, fantastic! You can still take it to the next level. A positive attitude is a critical component to transforming your life.

Historically, I have always been a positive person; however, when I completed the activity below, I was able to take positivity to the next level. This activity increased my awareness of how negative situations drain your energy and weaken your ability to remain positive. When you increase your awareness, you quickly develop a strategy to turn the situation around.

In Chapter 2, you ranked yourself on the 7 Strategies from "don't have a clue" to "kickin' butt." I will ask you to refer back to the rating for each strategy. Remember, it is not important that you rank yourself high or low. What is important is that you rank yourself accurately. It is just a starting point; it is where you are now. When you identify where you are now, you will be able to build a strategy to move forward.

How will you achieve your vision and dream to **Live Life Beyond the Laundry**?

First, you'll get an understanding of where you are in your life now (ranking on the continuum). Identify your challenges and obstacles, particularly what is getting in your way of living life to the fullest. You will then create powerful action items and goals to move you forward, setting milestones along the way to celebrate your success. Rank yourself one more time. Be totally honest.

Where are you now? (Power of a Positive Attitude)

(Clueless) 1   2   3   4   5   6   7   8   9   10 (Kickin' Butt)

Good. You now have a starting point. As you made your selection, I hope you were brutally honest. If you were not, the only person you hurt is yourself. The goal is not to shift from 2 to 8 overnight. This is too big of a step. You will become frustrated and overwhelmed, which leads to moving backward on the continuum. Your initial goal is to move forward two spaces. If you're currently at a 3, strive to shift to a 5. Continue to grow in that way. Daily action creates success. Results in life come from taking baby steps.

Before we learn more about the Power of a Positive Attitude activity, let's establish a clear perspective on the importance of making small incremental changes each day. Imagine you're a mountain climber and your dream is to reach the peak of Mount Everest. That is a big dream. Where do you begin? Can you simply stand at the base of the mountain and jump to the top? No, you have to place one foot in front of the other and climb to the peak step by step. This is the approach you will take throughout this book. Baby steps achieve ideal results for each strategy.

On average, it takes 30 days of consistent practice to form a new habit. There is nothing magical about 30 days; it is simply how the brain works. The brain is creating new neural and behavioral pathways to retrain your brain to do something. If you don't practice regularly and consistently, you won't benefit.

The good news is that many of the tools you learn throughout the book can easily be incorporated into your day. Before you know it, they will become part of your day, just like brushing your teeth.

The Power of a Positive Attitude Tool

The purpose of this tool is to increase your awareness of when you are thinking negatively about yourself or someone else. You will learn to reprogram your brain to be more positive. We all think negatively at some point or another. Pretend for a minute you are at a party and someone new walks into the room. What is the first thought that comes to your mind?

Many people think something negative. For example, you might criticize what the newcomer is wearing or what his or her hair looks like. Negative! You may not even realize you're doing this; however, it has a very powerful negative effect on you and the person you are criticizing, even though you just think it to yourself. This exercise reprograms your brain to turn negative thoughts around.

Step 1: Find a partner (friend, spouse, or child). Ask that person to help you conduct an experiment to learn more about the power of a positive attitude.

Step 2: Ask the person to extend his or her right arm out to the side (straight out from the shoulder).

Step 3: Place your left hand on the person's upper arm.

Step 4: Place your right hand on the person's forearm.

Step 5: Ask your assistant to think something positive about him/herself. The key is to think it, not say it out loud.

Step 6: As the person is thinking something positive, try to push down his or her arm. What happens?

Step 7: Now ask your assistant to think something negative about him/herself. Again, the key is to think, not say it out loud.

Step 8: As your assistant is thinking something negative, try to push down their arm. What happens?

Step 9: Wow, what did you learn?

Step 10: Repeat Step 6 to end this activity on a positive note.

Step 11: Now switch roles and complete Steps 1 through Step 10 so you can experience the power of positive versus negative thought. You must experience this activity to believe it. If you only read about it, your results will not be as great.

Reframe Attitude Tool (Ten-Day Challenge)

The purpose of the reframe attitude tool is to increase your awareness of when you are thinking negatively about yourself or someone else. You will learn to reprogram your brain to be more positive.

Step 1: Find a rubber band, silly band or stretchy bracelet.

Step 2: Place it on your wrist.

Step 3: Anytime you think something negative about yourself or someone else, switch the band to the other wrist.

Step 4: Do this for the next ten days.

Step 5: Write down what you observe.

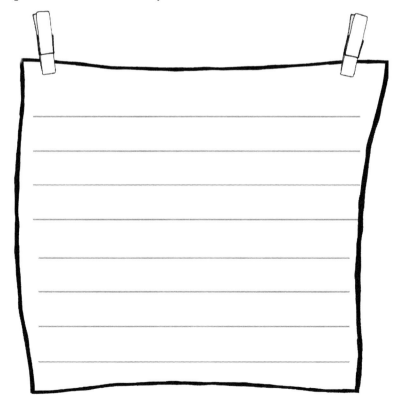

The reframe attitude tool will transform your life, even if you ranked yourself higher on the Where Are You Now continuum. When I originally completed this exercise, I ranked myself a 7 and I am now at a 9. The power of a positive attitude is amazing! It gives you the energy and strength to accomplish the change and transformation you want in your life.

Living Life Beyond the Laundry = Balancing Life

Studies have shown that, if you have a happy friend, your happiness increases by 15%. If your happy friend has a happy friend, it increases your happiness an additional 10%. If your happy friend's happy friend has a happy friend (even if you don't know any of them), your happiness goes up another 10%. ~Source unknown

A Very Bizzy Check In

Hey, it's Elizabeth again. This tool really works. It is truly amazing how much smoother my day goes when I am more positive. I also had my family do the Reframe Attitude Tool. It works! Everyone is talking a little nicer to each other and we are all happier with less stress.

My kids are having fun with it. I will hear one of them say "switch—that was negative." It has made a tremendous impact on the family time and the dynamics is our house. We have so much fun together, whereas before we tended to get on each other's nerves occasionally.

One other important lesson I learned is that I didn't realize how negative some of my friends are. Was I one of them? Well, not anymore. I have shared this tool with a couple of friends, and we're having fun with it. I have noticed that, when we go out together, we have more fun laughing versus trashing. I found the phrase below and it made me think of the changes I have begun to make in my life.

"There comes a time in your life, when you walk away from all the drama and people who create it. You surround yourself with people who make you laugh. Forget the bad, and focus on the good. Love the people who treat you right, pray for the ones who don't. Life is too short to be anything but happy. Falling down is part of life; getting back up is living." ~Jose N. Harris

Chapter 5

Strategy #1: "Me" Time

Life is really simple, but we insist on making it complicated. ~Confucius

Definition of "Me" Time: Time taken for yourself to relax or do something you enjoy.

Examples of "Me" Time: Garden, exercise, read, scrapbook, knit, go for a walk, have coffee with a friend, play with the dog, enjoy nature, and the list goes on. What do you truly enjoy?

Do you tend to push yourself too hard and strive for excellence? Do you have unrealistic daily expectations of yourself? Do you feel like your life has become a series of tasks to complete versus moments to enjoy? Are you convinced you can do it all, even if it creates a chaotic, stressful lifestyle? Do you secretly wish life would slow down a bit so you had a little more time for family fun, time with friends and an occasional date with your husband? If you answered YES to more than two of the above questions, you are beginning with the correct strategy—"Me" Time.

Many women believe that taking "Me" Time is selfish. I used to be one of them. Spending time on yourself is critical! Yes, as impossible as it may seem, taking "Me" Time is a necessity. If you do not take "Me" Time, you are likely to feel overwhelmed, stressed, and burned out, or even depressed. If you continue to neglect yourself, you will begin to notice your lack of an overall sense of joy and purpose in life. Your health may suffer, and it will likely become harder to tend to the needs of other people, priorities and responsibilities.

A common theme for women is: "I will take time for myself when my kids grow up." Don't wait that long. You will be a better mother, spouse and friend if you plan "Me" Time into your day. Even ten minutes a day helps. If you neglect tending to your own needs for relaxation, enjoyment and happiness, you are not at your peak. You are operating with your battery only partially charged.

On the flip side, the benefits of "Me" Time are tremendous. When you dedicate time to yourself each day, you have more energy for everything else. If you consistently build "Me" Time into your day for two weeks, you will begin to notice your stress level is lower, the days seem to run smoother, and you are more productive at work and at home.

The more you give to yourself, the better you are at giving to others. If you fear that taking "Me" Time will take away time from the time you have available for others—the opposite is actually true. You bring your best self to life's activities when you feel healthy, whole, and happy. The old saying, "Ain't nobody happy unless mama is happy" is true.

Somewhere in the busy day-to-day activities, you lost any time you ever had for yourself. You are so busy trying to please everyone else that you forget about yourself. You want to please your boss, want to be the best mom, spouse, friend—be the best you can be. This is an unrealistic expectation that results in stress, chaos, and exhaustion. Why are we so eager to please others at the expense of ourselves? Think about it, ladies.

Some signs to look for that indicate you need more "Me" Time:

- You feel like life is out of control (chaos and overwhelm).
- You feel undervalued and that no one appreciates everything you do.
- You feel busy and are not sure what you actually accomplish each day.
- You consistently put the needs of others before your own.
- You are at the bottom of your to-do list.

If you see yourself in any of the statements above, it's time for a change. The good news is that, with some creativity, persistence and dedication, you can recapture some critical "Me" Time.

Let's learn a little more about the importance of "Me" Time. It is

Live Life Beyond the Laundry Strategy #1 for a reason. If you don't learn to take time for yourself, Strategies #2 through #6 are a little more difficult to accomplish. You can certainly accomplish them, but they will be more challenging. So let's set you up for success from the beginning.

The typical response I get when I ask people about "Me" Time is—"I am too busy to take time for myself." My response is: "You are too busy not to plan time for yourself." "Me" Time is critical to reenergize and recharge your batteries. Batteries are more productive and efficient when fully charged. The same rule applies to you.

Let's dig a little deeper into the importance of "Me" Time. If you do not take time for yourself, you are unable to focus and be at your best for others. To put this in perspective, I would like to share a little story.

When you are flying on an airplane, the flight attendant has a safety message that must be given before the flight takes off. The flight attendant states, "Should we experience problems, an oxygen mask will drop from the ceiling. Please place your oxygen mask on before assisting others." What is the reason for this? You cannot take care of others if you have not first taken care of yourself.

Many women don't take care of themselves before others. They are the last item on their to-do list every day. I don't know about you, but I rarely get to the last item on my to-do list. The last item is reserved for, "It would be nice to complete but, if I don't get to it today, that's fine." That's not where we belong, ladies.

Now is the time to put the "Me" Time tool into action and understand how to make it work in your life. I will list the steps of the tool and then explain each step in detail.

Create "Me" Time Tool

Step 1: What do you like to do?

Write down what you enjoy doing. Make a list of ten to twenty activities (you started above; add more). Many people have trouble with this step. Life has become so stressed and chaotic that they can't remember what they enjoy doing anymore. Their lives have become so ingrained in taking care of everyone else but themselves that they have forgotten what they truly enjoy. Is that you?

Let's figure out what you enjoy doing. Think of it this way: If you had two hours to yourself tonight to do anything you wanted, what would you do? It cannot be laundry or housework; it must be something you love to do. Write it down in the space provided below.

If you still cannot figure it out, ask someone who knows you well. Ask your spouse, a parent or a good friend what you did for fun years ago. They may think it odd that you are asking them this question, but explain why you are asking and they might just benefit from the question as well. Write down what they say.

In this step, you are basically creating a "Me" Time menu, activities you have identified you enjoy. This is the list you refer to when you plan "Me" Time each day. Some of the activities might take ten minutes and some might take an hour. This gives you variety and choices.

If you are still feeling guilty about taking time for yourself, think of it this way. Your kids are watching and learning from you. You are teaching them it is okay to take time for themselves to relax and enjoy life. What a great lesson!

Example: "Me" Time Menu

- Remember the last time you had a good laugh and it will bring a smile to your face
- Soak in a warm tub with aromatherapy bath gel/salts surrounded by candles
- Get a massage, pedicure, facial (on a really good day, get all three!)
- Read a good book
- Take the dog for a walk around the block
- Call a great friend who makes you feel good
- Take a class to learn a new hobby such as knitting so now you have another fun activity for your "Me" Time menu
- Watch one of your favorite movies
- Exercise (This can only be on your "Me" Time menu if you truly love exercising. If you view exercising as a chore or something you have to do, it does not belong on this list. It is an essential part of self-care you must fit into your schedule. However, the activities on the "Me" Time menu are reserved only for the activities you truly enjoy.)

The possibilities are endless. Just ask yourself, "What do I enjoy and what do I feel like doing right now"?

Step 2: Why am I not taking time for myself?

Ask yourself: "Why am I not taking time for myself?" Be brutally honest and write it down! If you struggle with this, ask a friend or your spouse. I am sure they will have some ideas for you. During this step, you identify obstacles and challenges preventing you from implementing Strategy #1, "Me" Time, into your daily routine.

This is a critical step because we don't really understand why our days are so busy. They just are. Many of the activities we complete each day have become so routine that we just go through the motions on automatic pilot. Admit it, ladies, did you ever start the washing machine but could not remember if you put the detergent in the machine, and had to go back and check? Or have you ever driven around the block just to make sure you shut the garage door? This is called "automatic pilot."

By identifying your challenges and obstacles and asking yourself why you're so busy, you will be more successful in implementing this strategy. Listed below are some examples of obstacles and challenges I encountered when creating "Me" Time for myself.

- Kids' activities (taxi service)
- Laundry piling up
- I'm tired
- Picking up house
- Kids' homework
- Preparing meals
- Cleaning the kitchen
- Paying bills
- Cleaning the house

I'm sure you share some of the above obstacles. You might be thinking, "These are things I have to do." You are correct; however, there are strategies to make the above obstacles become more manageable. What are your obstacles?

Mommy guilt is another factor that acts as a barrier to accomplishing this strategy. Mommy guilt is like static cling; we all get it and we don't know where it comes from. The key is having the right tools on hand to know how to prevent it. What does mommy guilt look like for you? Besides lack of time, what triggers your mommy guilt?

As mentioned above, the benefits of taking "Me" Time are tremendous. Your kids will begin to notice you have more energy when you take time for yourself. What will you do with some of this extra energy? Spend time with them. They will love it. Give yourself permission to get over the mommy guilt, because this is something we do to ourselves.

You might say, I used to take time for myself, but I have just gotten too busy. Next month things will slow down and I will have more time. No, the time to start is today. You will not have more time next month if you don't implement this strategy. "Me" Time will not happen unless you make it happen.

As we proceed through the book, I will share information and stories about how I learned to manage the above challenges. You might identify a different obstacle in your life. Create a strategy to make it work for you, not against you. Remember, we need to get creative and persistent to make "Me" Time happen.

Here are a few games/strategies I have incorporated into my life to learn how to manage one of my obstacles, picking up the house. I try to make things fun so the family is more likely to participate willingly. When I feel like the house has gotten out of control—toys, shoes, backpacks, socks and just general clutter scattered about—I pick one of the games to get my house magically picked up in 20 minutes or less.

20-Minute Dash Game

The rules of the game are as follows:
- Everyone in the house participates
- Kitchen timer set for 20 minutes
- Fun, funky music playing
- TV off
- Ready, set, go
- Everyone goes around the house for 20 minutes picking up

Basket Time Game

The rules of the game are as follows:
- Everyone in the house participates
- Fun, funky music playing
- TV off
- Everyone has a mini-basket and walks from room to room picking up the items that belong to them. They then put everything in the basket away.

Power of 3 Game

The rules of the game are as follows:
- Everyone in the house participates
- Fun, funky music playing
- TV off
- Together walk from room to room
- Each person puts away three items in each room. (My husband and I can do about seven things in the time it takes my kids to do three)
- So, mathematically, 23 things get put away in each room

The end result of all three games:
- The house is picked up and the clutter is put away, for the most part.
- Created family time. The kids don't care what it is; they just like to spend time with you.
- The house is picked up in 20 minutes or less; this would have taken you at least 60 minutes on your own.
- You now have 40 minutes back. What will you do with those 40 minutes? Have "Me" Time and family time (look at your "Me" Time menu).

It all adds up, so set yourself up for success versus failure. Here is the trick; you have to accept the quality of work your kids (and husband) produce. Does it matter that your daughter folds the towels and puts them in the closet with all the unfolded edges facing out? Does it matter that your husband vacuums before he dusts?

(Okay, that one really does bother me.)

Let go of a little control here. The kids are learning and, remember, practice makes better. So let them practice and learn life skills. When life skills are taught from a young age, they stick! Your kids will be more successful in school and life. What a great gift!

Another way I create "Me" Time is by managing another obstacle: kids' activities (taxi service). I take the time spent waiting in the car to read a book or magazine… "Me" Time. Like I said, it all adds up.

Now it's your turn. Pick one of your challenges or obstacles and build a strategy to create "Me" Time. Get creative!

Step 3: For seven days, take ten minutes of "Me" Time each day.

Now that you have identified your obstacles and challenges and developed a few strategies to use time wisely, we are going to put "Me" Time into action. Here is your challenge. For the next seven days, take a minimum of ten minutes each day to do one of the activities listed in your "Me" Time menu (Step 1). Enjoy and have fun with it, and you will begin to reap the rewards of the effort in just seven days. You can do anything for seven days.

There is just one rule you must adhere to during this step.

Reducing the amount of time spent sleeping is not allowed to create "Me" Time. Sleeping six to eight hours each night is essential for you to **Live Life Beyond the Laundry**. Adequate sleep is essential to keeping energy levels up and stress levels down. Research indicates that lack of sleep leads to irritability, difficulty focusing or staying on task, and even headaches. Adhere to this rule to increase success in all 7 Strategies.

Step 4: How did this make you feel?

After those first seven days, write down how taking time for yourself made you feel. Do you feel happy, relaxed, productive, energized, guilty, or stressed? If you wrote down guilty, stressed or a different negative emotion, that is okay. Strategy #2 and Strategy #3 will help reduce the feelings of stress and guilt. However, continue to take ten minutes of "Me" Time each day.

If you wrote positive emotions, you are ready for Step 5, increasing the amount of "Me" Time. Whether negative or positive emotions were felt—either is fine—just keep moving forward. You will begin to shift to positive emotions if you are not already there. Remember, this is a journey and daily action creates results. Baby steps.

Step 5: Step it up a notch!

Now that you have successfully completed Step 4, try to increase the amount of "Me" Time you dedicate to yourself each day. For 23 more days, take a minimum of 20 minutes each day. The ultimate goal is to reach an average of 60 minutes each day. This is a stretch for many people. It may be that you take 30 minutes of "Me" Time during the week and enjoy the extra "Me" Time during the weekend. Remember, you are charging up your battery.

Step 6: Write it down

As you take these steps, write down how this made you feel (happy, productive, energized). When you consistently incorporate "Me" Time into your weekly activities, you begin to notice your productivity and happiness increase.

Step 7: Celebrate your success!

Treat yourself to something special to celebrate what you have achieved. Treat yourself to a pedicure, a new book, an afternoon with a friend. The activity is your choice; it is your celebration. Write down how you are going to celebrate your success below. This is an important step to **Live Life Beyond the Laundry**.

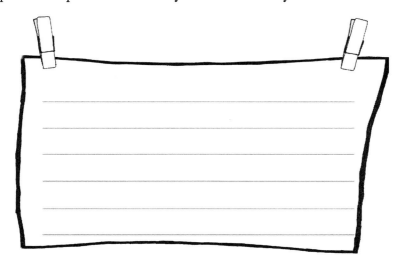

The key to success is consistency. It takes 30 days of consistent practice to create a new habit. Consistent means you do the new activity every day for 30 days. If you skip a day, begin again at day 1. Yes, I said begin again at day 1. We are rewiring your brain to live life a new way. To successfully sustain change, we must create new habits. This takes consistency and practice.

Living Life Beyond the Laundry = Balancing Life

If you think you can or can't, you're right. ~Henry Ford

A Very Bizzy Check In

Elizabeth again. I LOVE "Me" Time. It was hard to give myself permission to take ten minutes each day for myself. But I did it… I moved myself closer to the top of my to-do list. I feel great and I am actually getting more done around the house and spending quality time with the kids each day as a result.

My "Me" Time consists of reading a good book ten to twenty minutes before I go to bed each night. This makes me sleep well. I find I am not crabby anymore with my kids and husband. And my patience level has increased as well. The family loves the new me and so do I. I didn't like being crabby but couldn't help it. I am so excited about taking "Me" Time each day that I cannot imagine a day without it.

I'm proud to say I am taking it to the next level and increasing to 30 minutes a day. I posted my "Me" Time menu on the refrigerator to keep in sight as a reminder of the importance of "Me" Time.

Chapter 6

Strategy #2: Ask for Help

Three of the most powerful words in the English language
'Please help me.' ~Cathy Conheim

Definition: Not doing everything yourself…engaging in a conversation to ask someone to help you. In some cases, it may simply be delegating.

This is a very challenging strategy for many women. We feel the need to please people so we do everything, at our expense, just to make someone else's life easier. Why do we do that? We all have good reasons, some of which could possibly be classified as excuses. Let's take a look at some of the reasons.

Top Reasons (Excuses)

- It is easier and quicker to do it myself.
- If I let them do it, I will either have to redo it or I'll have to fix their mistakes.
- I don't trust them to get it done.
- My husband/kids are too busy; I don't want to bother them.
- I cannot ask my friends to help me with that. I should be able to do it myself. They are busy, too.

What are your reasons? (add to the list)

Who told you that you had to do everything on your own? Society, your mother, you? We create expectations for ourselves that we simply cannot achieve. It is simply impossible to do it all. We may try, but this is where stress and chaos bloom. We need to work together and help each other out, but where do we begin?

As I mentioned above, this is a very common problem for women. We feel guilty if we ask for help. Yes, I said it again—GUILTY. As I conduct presentations and coach busy working women, this word comes out of their mouths often. Give yourself permission to move beyond guilt; it is just an excuse.

Let's explore why it is so important to ask for help or to delegate. Let's talk a little about how our inability to ask for help hurts others.

Problem – Solution – Success Tool

The purpose of this tool is to shift your thoughts and increase your confidence to ask for help…without GUILT.

You will learn to identify a problem, find a solution, and then celebrate your success. When you celebrate your success, it creates an awareness of how well the solution worked. Below are some typical problems associated with this tool.

The Problem: Our Children

Where do I begin? It is our job as parents to teach our children life skills. If you do not teach your kids how to clean, cook, manage their time and ask for help, who is going to—their freshman college roommate? Probably not, because they did not learn these life skills as children, either. We have created an extremely dependent generation. Why did we do this? Because it was just easier to do it ourselves or because our kids are so busy that we don't want to add another responsibility to their busy lives. (Hello…you are busy and stressed as well!)

When we decide to do everything ourselves, we don't teach our children essential life skills or time management. A friend of mine actually had to teach her son how to change the toilet paper roll when he moved into his college apartment. In the first 19 years of his life, she did not think to teach him how to do this. Not learning essential life skills leads to stress, chaos and embarrassment in your children's adult lives.

The Solution:

Our children can help out around the house. They may grumble about it at first; however, they will soon realize the household runs smoother when everyone contributes. Less chaos! How can I make this work?

Divide and conquer tool

Step 1: Make a list of everything you do around the house.

Step 2: Circle the items you want to be responsible for. These may be tasks you want completed a certain way and are unwilling to compromise your standards.

Step 3: Sit down with the family (kids and significant other). Show them the remainder of the list (tasks you are willing to accept less than perfect results for).

Step 4: Ask them if there are a couple of items they think they could be responsible for. It is imperative that you take the ages of your kids into consideration during the selection process. However, if you let them choose, they are more likely to take responsibility for this task.

Step 5: Together decide on when and how each task should be completed. Type up the list and post it in a central location of the house.

Step 6: Explain the WIFM (What's in it for me). When the family understands that you will have more time for them and will be happier, they are more likely to contribute.

Step 7: Catch them being good. Once in a while when you see them doing the task, thank them for helping out. For example, yesterday my son was cleaning out the dishwasher and then put the dirty dishes in without being asked. My husband caught him being good and thanked him. End result: a smile on my son's face, priceless.

Step 8: Celebrate your success. After a few week of successful implementation have a fun family activity.

Step 9: Review the plan occasionally to see if any modifications are required.

This exercise can be applied at home and at work. This is called teamwork.

You may choose to pay an allowance to reinforce and reward their added effort, but this is optional. For some families an allowance works great, and some families feel it is just part of their family contribution. Either works. Just keep it consistent.

Success Story:

My 5th grader loves to help cook dinner. The other night we were making Sloppy Joes. Actually, he was making Sloppy Joes and I was supervising. He thought I was just visiting with him. He was telling me how important it is to make cooking fun as he drew a smiley face with the catsup on the cooked ground beef. He was so proud of himself for making dinner. What life lessons were taught during this little story?

- How to prepare a meal.
- The importance of having fun and not taking life too seriously.
- The importance of spending quality time with family members.
- Making a contribution to the household.
- Responsibility.

All this, and I was able to spend quality time with my child. Make an effort to include your children in household activities. So many fun memories will be created.

Success Story:

My sister has successfully implemented the divide-and-conquer tool into her life for at least two years. A few years back, she sat down with her husband and two kids. She had made a list of all the household chores that needed to be completed over the course of the week. Based on what chores were age-appropriate for her kids, they made chore lists A and B. The kids are assigned a chore list each week and then swap the next. Within the chore list, they can trade and negotiate but, ultimately, each child is responsible for his or her own list that week. She asked each child to pick five chores and they created a fun chart and laminated it. The kids trade the chore list back and forth week by week. This creates weekly variety and no one person is stuck folding the socks every week. What has she accomplished? Less stress and responsibility for her and increased responsibilities for her kids, all while teaching valuable life skills.

The Problem: Our Friends

We feel guilty asking our friends for help because they are busy. Think about it this way, when we don't ask our friends for help they feel guilty asking us for help. Thus the circle of guilt is created. Guess what…they need help just as bad as you do. It is a vicious circle of guilt, stress and chaos. Create a solid relationship with a friend where you help each other out to make life just a little easier. Did you know that if you help each other out, you will both have more time? Imagine that!

The Solution:

Create a strategic parent partnership. Identify a friend or a parent of one of your children's best friends, and discuss how you can help each other out. The first step might be to create car pools, but you have to take it to the next level. You can call this friend to help you out with anything any time. Let's say you have a meeting you know is going to run late tonight and Suzy needs to be picked up from piano lessons. What do you do? Call your strategic parent partner and have her pick Suzy up if it works for her. You simply help each other out. There are a few rules to create a successful parent partnership.

Rule 1: No guilt (this must be from both sides of the partnership).

Rule 2: Don't abuse the relationship (do your part to make it a success).

Rule 3: Communicate what is working and what is not, and figure out a solution to maintain your partnership.

Rule 4: No keeping track. Sometimes you will need a bit more help, and sometimes your strategic parent partner needs more. We all have busier times in our lives. If one of the parent partners begins to take advantage, go back to Rule 3 and communicate.

Rule 5: If it is not working, just find a different strategic parent partner. I have created three strategic parent partnerships over the years, one for each of my children. I have two still in place. The third one did not fail. Things just changed and life goes on. If something is not working, change it. Blessed are the flexible, for they shall not be bent out of shape.

Success Story: I am very proud of my success in this area.

I have one strategic parent partnership that was created when my daughter was in 3rd grade. She is now a freshman in college. My strategic parent partner and I helped each other out in many ways as our girls grew up, driving to piano lessons, answering homework questions, making a poodle skirt for fifties day at school, resolving high school drama issues, and the list goes on and on. The key to success: no guilt, no keeping track and strong communication. I now have a great friend and we still schedule time with each other to celebrate our success.

I have another strategic parent partnership that was created when my son was one. He's now a 9th grader. We helped each other out in many ways as our boys grew up, picking up at daycare, and driving to summer camps. We would even dump our kids on each other when our other kids had sleepovers planned and we wanted a date night with our husbands. The key to success: no guilt, no keeping track, and strong communication. I now have a great friend and my son has a best friend and second mom for life.

The Problem: Our Significant Others

Did you know they get just as frustrated with us as we do with them? We assume they can read our minds. We send them telepathic messages to empty the dishwasher, pick up the house and do a load of laundry, and then get frustrated and mad when they don't. We forget the key ingredient: ask. If we ask, they will help out.

The Solution:

Strong communication and collaboration. Create a household success plan and learn to ask for help from your spouse and children when you need it. I repeat: they cannot read your mind and they have different priorities. I get stressed when my kitchen counter becomes the dumping ground for everyone's miscellaneous items. So I told my husband that, and now he is more aware and just puts things away. For him, it is the garage. He gets frustrated when I place items in the garage that do not belong: empty shoe boxes, for example. Too bad it took us 15 years of marriage to tell each other that.

Remember to celebrate your success, and have a fun date night when you successfully create and implement this plan.

Success Story:

When my youngest child was two, I worked part-time and developed the habit of doing everything around the house myself. It just seemed easier and everything was done how and when I wanted. After about a year, my job required I go back to work full-time. I thought I could continue the pace at home by myself. I began to feel stressed, tired, and my life was very chaotic. It dawned on me I needed to ask for help.

One night I sat my husband down and politely explained to him that I could not do this all on my own and was surprised that he said he would help more. His commitment to help more around the house was a relief. I felt like 1,000 pounds had fallen off my shoulders.

The timing of this conversation was crucial to its success. I planned it for a time when the household was calm and we weren't in a rush to get somewhere. I explained the situation and how I was feeling, and I asked for help. The conversation did not involve yelling, accusations or lecturing. Simply stating I couldn't do everything and needed some help was not enough, though; we developed a plan together and put it into action.

I learned two lessons from this experience. First, we must ask because our spouses cannot read our minds; they just think we're getting crabby or bitc&%. Second, they do not see the messes we see. I know this for a fact, as I would occasionally conduct an experiment to see how long a dirty sock or underwear would sit in the hallway until someone picked it up. That someone was usually me, and I could typically only stand it for about four days.

My husband and I have increased our communication and we both ask for help when we need it from each other. We have times during our work schedules that are a bit busier. In March and November, I have a heavy teaching schedule, so I just mention it to him and he steps it up a bit around the house by cleaning the kitchen more often. He knows this is my least favorite chore. The power of communication.

The Problem: You

When you do everything yourself, you create stress, chaos and anxiety. This is not healthy.

Let's learn a little more about stress. Stress is a normal physical response to events that make you feel threatened. When you sense danger, real or imagined, the body's defenses kick into high gear in a rapid, automatic process known as the "fight-or-flight" reaction, or the stress response. Your body is not meant to function at this heightened reactive state.

The stress response is the body's way of protecting you. Some stress is okay. It is the body's way of telling you to increase your senses and get ready to perform. Too much stress is unhealthy. It reduces your productivity, affects your mood, quality of life and your relationships.

Keep this in mind: Stress is caused by positive as well as negative events. A wedding, birth of a baby or even just packing for vacation are all positive events that cause stress. The important factor is that you recognize what is causing your stress and create a strategy to move forward.

Solution:

Learn to recognize signs that you are becoming stressed so you can create a plan and put it into action. Once you are aware of what your stress signals are, it is easier to create a plan and put it into action. This will shift you from chaos to calm faster.

Many people describe the chaotic, stressful feeling as standing in the middle of the room, spinning and not knowing how to stop, or that they are going through a revolving door and are not sure where it will open and what they will encounter.

Learn to recognize your stress symptoms. The following table lists some of the common warning signs and symptoms of stress. The more signs and symptoms you notice in yourself, the closer you may be to stress overload. According to helpguide.org, the following are some of the typical signs people experience: Circle the ones that apply to you.

Stress Warning Signs and Symptoms

Cognitive Symptoms	Emotional Symptoms
• Memory problems • Inability to concentrate • Poor judgment • Seeing only the negative • Anxious or racing thoughts • Constant worrying	• Moodiness • Irritability or short temper • Agitation, inability to relax • Feeling overwhelmed • Sense of loneliness and isolation • Depression or general unhappiness
Physical Symptoms	Behavioral Symptoms
• Aches and pains • Diarrhea or constipation • Nausea, dizziness • Chest pain, rapid heartbeat • Frequent colds	• Eating more or less • Sleeping too much or too little • Isolating yourself from others • Procrastinating or neglecting responsibilities • Using alcohol, cigarettes, or drugs to relax • Nervous habits (e.g. nail biting, pacing)

Keep in mind that the signs and symptoms of stress can also be caused by other psychological and medical problems. If you're experiencing any of the warning signs of stress, it's important to see a doctor for a full evaluation. Your doctor can help you determine whether your symptoms are stress-related.

Solution:

Now that we have identified the effects of too much stress, let's learn techniques to manage stress. One of the key components to reducing stress is asking for help. Below are techniques and activities to explore to reduce your stress.

- Ask for help
- Yoga
- Deep breathing
- Exercise
- Adequate sleep (6 to 8 hours)
- Journaling (will help you identify what is creating stress)
- Learning to say NO (Strategy #3)
- Managing your never-ending to-do list (Strategy #4)

Strategy #2, ask for help, will have a direct impact on your stress level. Why would you not take time to make this change in your life immediately? I can guarantee you it will take work and effort, and I can guarantee you it will be worth it.

Success Story:

The success story for this section is me. I now ask for help versus feeling stressed or chaotic. Why spend five hours stressing out about something I am not really sure how to do if I can ask an expert? For example, I really don't enjoy or fully understand everything in QuickBooks. Yes, I can do the basic and easy tasks but, instead of spending hours learning on my own, I asked the expert. I have a friend who is great at it, and she taught me the tips and tricks of QuickBooks. I happen to be great at organizing, so I helped her organize her office.

When do you struggle to ask for help? Identify the situation and develop a solution to successfully move you through this obstacle. If you struggle to come up with a solution to the problem, ask for help.

As busy women, we think we can do it all by ourselves. Admit it, girls, we need to help each other out. Share this strategy with all your friends and family. Everyone will reap the rewards.

Living Life Beyond the Laundry = Balancing Life

It is so much friendlier with 2. ~Winnie the Pooh

A Very Bizzy Check In

Hey, it's Bizzy again, asking for help. OMG, this is so hard. I am so used to doing it myself. I have done it that way for so many years. But I guess that is why everyone calls me Bizzy versus Elizabeth. I'm working on this strategy; however, I have more work to do. I now understand why asking for help is so important. I need to do it more often.

The other night, I sat my family down over ice cream sundaes (ice cream, hot fudge, sprinkles and tons of whipped cream) to ask for help. I thought I had to butter them up with extra gooey ice cream sundaes to get them to agree. To my amazement, they were willing to take on the responsibility of a couple of chores around the house. The hardest thing for me was giving up control of how the towels were folded. We split up the household responsibilities and, so far, after week one, everyone is going great.

I guess I don't have to do everything. I'll keep working on this strategy because I just want to be Elizabeth again.

Chapter 7

Chaos Reduction Strategy #3:
NO is Not a Four Letter Word

Half of the troubles of this life can be traced to saying "Yes"
too quickly and not saying "No" soon enough. ~Josh Billings

Definition: No—A word used to express refusal in response to a question or request.

This is a very difficult strategy for women to implement because we habitually say YES to the requests and demands people make. We do this because we think it is expected of us, and we want to live up to others' expectations. Why should we sacrifice ourselves just to please others?

We were raised (thanks, Mom) to please others and put ourselves second or, even worse, last. When you say YES to everything, it makes you feel overwhelmed and over-committed. In other words, busy and chaotic. Over time, this is harmful to your mental and physical health.

Don't create this for yourself. Yes, I said, don't create this for yourself. Create the life you live. Remember: NO is a complete sentence.

When I first began working on this strategy, I was a 1—clueless. I can now proudly say I am consistently an 8…almost to kickin' butt. It took some work to get there, but it has made a tremendous difference in my life. Too bad I didn't learn about this strategy 15 years ago, but better late than never.

I used to be Miss Volunteer (there was even a sparkly sash and crown I wore). Go ask Christy; she'll do it. If you have been crowned Miss Volunteer, you are ready to put this strategy into action. Your survival depends on it. The key to success is simplifying your life to minimize stress and chaos. Begin now!

Don't get me wrong. It is still important to volunteer and become involved in your community. Community involvement creates new friendships and gives you a tremendous amount of happiness and pride (and also opportunities to create strategic parent partnerships). The key is to volunteer for only the committees and events you truly want to join. When you truly want to join a committee or event, you bring your "A" game. You will give 150%!

If you volunteer for something you really don't want to do, but feel like you SHOULD, you will bring your "holy crap! I cannot believe I have one more thing to do" game.

This rule even applies when your friends invite you to do something. For example, a friend calls and invites you to girls' night out. You really have not seen this friend for a while and feel like you SHOULD go. But you've had a really busy week and just want to be home spending quality time with your family. What will you do?

You feel guilty if you say YES to the friend because you are then ignoring your family. If you say NO, you also feel guilty because you are disappointing your friend. It is a double-edge sword. Oh, the GUILT! Get over it, ladies, do what will make you the happiest. Do what you want to do. Simply tell your friend thanks for the invite, but it just isn't going to work out that night.

Unfortunately, most of us say, "No, that is not going to work for me, I have not been home most of the week, and the kids have been bugging me to make cookies. I have already told them later three times this week. So I really need to stay home. I feel bad that I cannot make it work because we haven't hung out for a couple of months. However, I need to spend time with the kids. Sorry, let's do it next week."

Slow down. Did you really need to say all that? NO! All you need to say is "Thanks for the invite, but that won't work for me tonight." Then shut your mouth. If it is too hard to shut your mouth, imagine a piece of duct tape over your mouth. Nobody really cares about all that other junk. That is you trying to justify your decision and ease your guilt.

When I started saying NO, I found that I enjoyed the time I spent with my family and friends even more. It was quality time. Quality time is more important than quantity of time. I also noticed I enjoyed the committees and community activities I was involved with even more. I was doing what I loved versus what I felt I should or ought to do.

Another option is to offer an alternative to the request. For example, when someone asks you to chair the school carnival (like you have for the last few years), you can instead volunteer to be on the committee for the fall fund-raising event.

Just remember to always ask yourself if you really want to do this. If your answer is YES, then go for it. If your answer is, you really don't want to, but you feel like you should, say NO, that is not going to work for me right now. Don't explain. As women, we feel the need to justify the access we give others to our time. Remember you can say NO without feeling guilty. The moral of the story is: don't SHOULD on yourself.

As mentioned earlier, it is good to volunteer, but make the right choices. Give back to the community and spend time with friends. However, choose activities you enjoy. You will bring more excitement and energy to the group you are working or socializing with if you are truly invested in the activity. You will look forward to doing what is on your schedule versus dreading it. Therefore, say YES to what you are truly passionate about, and NO to what you feel like you SHOULD do. Don't SHOULD on yourself.

So where do you begin? How do you say NO? More than likely you already have activities in your schedule you don't enjoy. They deplete your energy and contribute to your busy, chaotic life. You need to minimize the daily activities that do not nourish you.

This is one of my best success tips. When I give presentations and see people six, nine or even twelve months later, they will tell me, "Christy, I am not SHOULDING on myself anymore." This is when I know a tool truly works. Saying NO more often reduces the chaos in your life.

Are you thinking this is easier said than done? You can do it. Find the courage to give it a try. When I first learned this technique, I was sailing along great until a good friend of mine asked me to be on a committee that I really did not want to be on. I thought about it and then realized I was being tested. So I asked myself if I really wanted to join this committee. My answer was "NO, but I SHOULD." I did not "SHOULD" on myself and instead said "No, that is not going to work for me. Thanks for thinking of me." And, guess what, she said okay and just asked someone else. Truly amazing!

There are two areas of focus to fully implement this strategy: what is already in your life and future requests. The activities below will teach you how to handle both. Give it a try. To fully implement this strategy, you need to learn about and implement both tools.

Don't SHOULD on Yourself Tool

The purpose of this tool is to teach you how to say YES when you really want to say YES, and NO when you really want to say NO.

Step 1: Next time someone asks you to do something or to join something, think before you reply.

Step 2: Ask yourself: "Do I want to do this?"

Step 3: If you answer, "Yes, I want to do this," say YES.

Step 4: If your answer is, "I ought to or I SHOULD," say NO.

Step 5: Remember, don't SHOULD on yourself.

Step 6: Be aware of the times when you say YES when you really wanted say NO. Is there a common theme? For example, is a good friend asking you? Is it harder to say NO to her than it is to say NO to the PTA president? If these are the same people, you are up for a big challenge! But remember this: It gets easier each time NO comes out of your mouth.

Activity Elimination Tool

The purpose of this tool is to eliminate obligation and commitments from your schedule that you do not enjoy. They simply do not add value to your life.

During this activity, we are going analyze what activities and commitments you already have in your life. This exercise will take roughly 30 minutes to complete and may take up to a year to fully implement. We are going to identify the activities and commitments you want to keep and shed the ones you don't enjoy. The reason I say it may take up to a year to fully implement is that some committees have a time frame or an event deadline you must fulfill. Create your exit strategy today and put it into action.

This is a tool I teach 80% of my coaching clients. One of the main sources of chaos is too many obligations and commitments. This is part of why you feel so busy. Many people have every minute of every day scheduled. Slow down and enjoy life. Remember life was meant to be enjoyed, not tolerated. So let's begin.

Step 1: Fill out the first column of the chart below by listing all responsibilities and activities you are involved in. I have given you a few examples to get you started. People are amazed by how long this list is. Use an extra sheet of paper if you need more space.

Step 2: Review the list and place an X in the column this activity belongs.
- Need to Do: There are certain activities in life we have to do. They are responsibilities.
- Want to Do: You love this activity and it brings happiness and energy to life.
- Should on Myself: I wish I did not have to do this, but I said YES so I guess I have to. This creates so much stress and chaos in my life.

Activity	Need to Do	Want to Do	Should Do (end date)
School Carnival Committee			X (end 4-1)
Girl Scout Leader		X	
Go to work	X		

Step 3: Create an exit strategy to eliminate the Should Do actives from your life. Begin this step today. Many committees have a time commitment due to an event deadline or term required on a board. Create your exit strategy and put it into action so you don't accidentally get signed up for another year or term.

Step 4: On all future requests, utilize the Don't SHOULD on Yourself Tool. Notice when you say YES and you really want to say NO. Don't SHOULD on yourself! Do not skip step 4. It will help you understand WHY you say YES and will help you build powerful strategies to remove the Should Do activities from your list. Write down the date of your exit from the Should Do item.

Example Ideas to remove "Should Do" activities

1. At the next PTA meeting, tell members you are no longer able to help with the carnival. Say you'll be happy to train someone to create a smooth transition for your responsibilities. Don't cave when they beg you to do just one more year. Be strong.

2. You are on the board for the hockey association and do not enjoy this activity. You have placed it in the Should Do activity column. Next time the board meets, announce that you will be resigning after this season ends. This will give them plenty of time to find a replacement.

3. You volunteer every Wednesday afternoon in your child's room. The teacher has come to depend on you; however, you no longer have the time to dedicate every Wednesday. Sit down with the teacher and explain that your schedule has changed. Let the teacher know that, starting after Christmas break, you will not be able to volunteer every week. Don't over-explain why; just let the teacher know it no longer fits into your schedule. Because you enjoy this activity, let the teacher know you're available every other week.

4. What are your strategies? Write below.

This takes us back to consistency. Consistency is the key to success. It takes 30 days of consistent practice to create a new habit. Consistency means you do the new activity every day for 30 days. If you skip a day, begin again at Day 1. We are rewiring your brain to live life a new way. To successfully sustain change, we must create new habits. This takes consistency and practice.

After 90 days of consistent practice, the new habit is a part of your daily life, similar to brushing your teeth. You cannot imagine living your day without it. The upfront daily actions have a tremendous reward for your quality of life. Living life beyond the laundry starts with the action you take.

Living Life Beyond the Laundry = Balancing Life

People are so busy knocking themselves out trying to do everything they think they should do, they never get around to do what they want to do. ~Kathleen Winsor

A Very Bizzy Check In

Hey, it's Bizzy again. When I first read about this strategy, I was completely overwhelmed. My list of activities and commitments was endless. But then I thought to myself, Strategy #1 and #2 have made such a difference in my life. I need to try Strategy #3. What have I got to lose?

I made the list of my activities and commitments, then identified three in the SHOULD column that I could eliminate immediately. I eliminated them and it felt fantastic. This gave me the momentum to work on the rest of the SHOULD list, and I am proud to say I have an exit strategy for every item in the SHOULD column. A couple of them will take me a year to implement, but I created the strategy to move forward.

Yay, me! I think I need to celebrate my success. I worked hard on this strategy. I think this deserves a spa day!

Chapter 8

Strategy #4: Focused Balancing Act

I learned that we can do anything, but we can't do everything... at least not at the same time. So think of your priorities, not in terms of what activities you do, but when you do them. Timing is everything. ~Dan Millman

Definition: Focused Balancing Act—To accomplish more than what you currently do in a day; in other words managing your time wisely (time management).

Strategy #4 includes several tools that will improve your time management skills. Many of the tools can be applied both at home and work. There are only 1,440 minutes in a day and, once you use them, they are gone. When you really think about it, time is the only commodity we cannot purchase more of, so use your time wisely. Most people are overwhelmed with too much to do and too little time to do it in. Chaos is a choice! Calm is a choice!

Learning to properly manage time is a very important success factor that allows you to **Live Life Beyond the Laundry.** It is critical to successfully managing your work and home life. Many women I talk to say, "I just want to have balance in my life." Well, ladies, sorry to break the news to you, but complete work/balance is an unrealistic expectation. You will never get because there it is not a destination. Reframe your thinking and phrase it like this: I want to learn the tools to strive for balancing my life. It is all a balancing act and, when you use the correct tools, you can balance.

Balancing life is comparable to a tightrope walker. A tightrope walker must use the balancing pole (tool) to move forward successfully with each step (daily action creates results). It takes focus every step of the way to reach the other side of the tightrope (your day). The tightrope walker is balancing, not balanced.

Work/life balance is not a destination; it is the life we lead. It takes work every day to live a life of balancing or, as I call it, to **Live Life Beyond the Laundry**. You may be thinking you don't have any time for more work. It is not more work if you learn to use the tools properly. When Strategy #4 is integrated into your life, you will have 45 to 60 minutes more each day.

What would you do with an extra 45 to 60 minutes each day? How about more "Me" Time, family time, and time with friends. When you begin to feel less busy, overwhelmed and chaotic, you learn to enjoy life, or to **Live Life Beyond the Laundry**. I challenge you to implement at least three of the tools below into your life for the next 30 days. This is what it takes to create the extra 45 to 60 minutes in your day.

This takes us back to consistency. The key to success is consistency. It takes 30 days of consistent practice to create a new habit. Consistent means you do the new activity every day for 30 days. If you skip a day, begin again at Day 1. We are rewiring your brain to live life a new way. To successfully sustain change, we must create new habits. This takes consistency and practice.

After 90 days of consistent practice, the new habit becomes a part of your daily life, similar to brushing your teeth. You cannot imagine living your day without it. The upfront daily actions and work have a tremendous reward for your quality of life.

Success Story:

I conducted a training session on this topic for a business in town. When training is completed, participants always leave with action items to implement. This particular training session happened during the summer. The training went great and all participants embraced the action items to get more done in less time.

About six weeks after the training, I saw one of the participants and asked her how things were going. She said, "Christy, I am great. I feel like I am getting so much done and I am not as busy and overwhelmed as I was over the summer. It must be the change of seasons and that fall is here." I then asked her, "Have you been working on your action items from the training?" She said, "Yes, they work great." I then explained to her it was not the change in seasons that was creating the feeling of getting more done and reducing overwhelm and chaos. It was the fact that she had created new habits by consistently implementing Strategy #4.

It takes time to recognize the results of your work. It's not a magic spell that can be cast upon you to create this overnight. If you do the work, you will reap the reward. I guarantee it. It will not always feel like work. Eventually, it will transition into how you live. Planning your day will be just as important as brushing your teeth. You won't be able to imagine a day without either.

This strategy works. This is one of the first tools I share with the busy working women I coach. Once they begin using this tool consistently, they see results. I can always tell if they have stopped using the tool. They show up at their coaching sessions stressed and frustrated. I always ask, "Have you been power planning ten minutes a day?" The answer is almost always NO. Source of stress and chaos revealed. They have stopped planning.

Studies indicate that one minute of planning equates to ten minutes of productivity. In theory, then, if you plan for ten minutes each day, you will have 100 extra minutes of productivity each day. This is based on consistency and does not happen overnight. After about four weeks of consistent use, you will begin to notice you are getting more done and not feeling as stressed or chaotic.

Let's learn more about the Balancing Act strategy and how to make it work in your life.

Did you know…an average person who develops the habit of setting clear priorities each day and getting the most important task done first will run circles around a genius? ~Source Unknown

Power Plan Tool

The purpose of this tool is to provide you with a game plan for the day, teach you how to set realistic expectations, and how to increase your sense of accomplishment. Set yourself up for success instead of failure each day.

Women pride themselves on how much they can accomplish in a day by multi-tasking; however, several studies have been done over the past decade that indicate exactly the opposite. Multi-tasking creates chaos, stress and anxiety, resulting in a feeling that you did not accomplish much during the day.

What exactly is multi-tasking? Multi-tasking is shorthand for a woman's attempt to do simultaneously as many things as possible, as quickly as possible. The opposite of multi-tasking is focus. Focus is concentrating on one activity until it is complete or significant progress has been made toward a portion of the activity. Several studies indicate that, when people focus on individual tasks instead of attempting to multi-task, they accomplish more.

To avoid the chaos of multi-tasking, you must learn to focus. How do you do that? You would think the ability to focus on one task is a natural ability we have, but it isn't. Like all the other habits you are implementing into this new lifestyle, focusing on one task at a time is a habit you have to develop.

In one of the many letters he wrote to his son in the 1740s, Lord Chesterfield offered the following advice: "There is time enough for everything in the course of the day if you do but one thing at once, but there is not time enough in the year if you will do two things at a time."

Note: Use electronic planner, paper planner or notebook for this exercise.

Step 1: At the end of your work day, take the last ten minutes of the day to create a plan for tomorrow: details of the next day. You can use this technique for planning at home as well. This is called your Power Plan time.

Benefit: You leave work at work and enjoy your home life, and vice versa. You leave home at home and are fully present, engaged and productive at work.

Tip: Don't schedule every hour of the day. Things happen that are out of our control. For example, a customer walks in to make a big purchase or your manager asks for a report for his afternoon meeting. Neither of these distractions were in your plan but, because you have built flexibility into your schedule, things like this will not derail you. This is called fluff time. Built-in flexibility allows you catch up time during the day.

*Blessed are the flexible for they shall not
be bent out of shape. ~source unknown*

Step 2: Each day, circle the most difficult task you need to complete and schedule it first thing in the morning. This is the task you really don't want to do but have to do. If you circle this task each day and schedule it first thing in the morning, you will not think about it all day long. Just check it off and get it done. This will make the balance of your day more productive.

Time management guru Brian Tracy refers to this as "eating your frog." He says your frog is the most difficult task you have to complete each day. If the first thing you do each day is eat your frog, you won't have to look at it all day.

Step 3: Each Friday, take the last ten minutes of the work day to power plan out what the next week looks like. You are not filling in all the details of the week; it's just an overview. It allows you to see what is coming up next week. For example, you might see that Wednesday afternoon is completely open, free from all meetings. You have a project deadline coming up, so schedule it into Wednesday afternoon when you have time. Schedule this time before someone else at work schedules it for you with another meeting.

Benefit: You leave work at work and enjoy your home life over the weekend. Your family will appreciate this step. The quality of the time spent with your family over the weekend will be very rewarding.

Success Story:

I shared this tool with a friend of mine this past March, and she shared with me a few months later how dramatic the change was in her schedule. She told me it felt like she was getting a lot more done. She also thought it had been the change in the seasons, but when I asked her if she had been doing her power plan each day, the light bulb came on. She was feeling the results of her planning and it had just become a new habit for her, an effortless part of her day.

Success Story:

I created a power plan and put it into action to create this book. In the final week before I sent the manuscript to my editor, I blocked out the entire week with the exception of "Me" Time, family time, and exercise time. This provided clear and dedicated focus.

Below are a series of mini-tools I utilize each week or month to catch up and keep on track. Use these tools or modify them to meet the unique needs of your family. Or better yet, create your own and share them with me at Christy@SimplyBalancedCoaching.com. I love to hear about your success.

Mini-Tool Clustering

The purpose of this tool is to provide focus and efficiency to activities that are similar in nature. Paying bills as they come in is not an efficient use of time. Sit down and pay them a couple of times a month or, better yet, set up bill pay so it just happens automatically. This is a tool I utilize daily to get more done in less time. It involves time blocking and planning to be successful.

***Mini-Tool: Right Turn Errands
- Create a list of errands you need to make around town.
- Complete the errands by making right turns only. (Yes, you may occasionally have to make a left turn. However, each left turn adds roughly five to ten minutes to the time it takes to complete your errands). Now, you may be laughing; however, try it and see for yourself. UPS schedules delivery routes based on this approach.

***Mini-Tool: Paper and a Chick Flick
We all have that pile of paper that stacks up over time:
1. Find a good chick flick, one you have already seen but just love watching.
2. Stack up all the papers on a table, hit the play button, and start at the top of the stack.
3. Don't save anything for later. Just complete whatever needs to be done.
4. You will be amazed how much you accomplish by the time the movie is over.

***Mini-Tool: Friday Taskmaster
- I time-block a couple of hours on Friday to catch up whatever I can so I can have a great weekend with family and friends. NOTE: You don't have to use Fridays. If Fridays don't work, pick a different time.
- Thursday night or Saturday morning are other great task-master times. The point is, you focus and get everything done in a chunk of time so you can enjoy the rest of the weekend. Some of the things include paying bills, grocery shopping and laundry.

Feel free to create your own mini-tools. The goal of a mini-tool is to create focused, dedicated time to accomplish more in less time, leaving extra time for what's really important in life.

Time management is making small changes that add up over the course of the day, week and month. When you consistently practice good time management skills, your life begins to move smoother with less chaos and stress. This allows you to **Live Life Beyond The Laundry**.

Time Study Tool

The purpose of this tool it to identify activities you need to spend less time on or spend more time on. This increases productivity and efficiency.

Step #1: For the next seven days, complete the time study below. I have provided a table for the first three days. Use a note book, Excel spread sheet, or the provided pages at the back of this book for days four through seven.

The ultimate goal of this study is to learn how to manage your time both at work and at home. Part of this process includes completing a time study. For the next seven days, please record your activities accurately. Use this study for the following steps. Remember to be brutally honest. If you shop online or play video games for three hours one day, put it down. Even record how long you sleep.

Time	Day 1	Day 2	Day 3
5:30 AM			
6:00 AM			
6:30 AM			
7:00 AM			
7:30 AM			
8:00 AM			
8:30 AM			
9:00 AM			
9:30 AM			
10:00 AM			
10:30 AM			
11:00 AM			
11:30 AM			
12:00 PM			
12:30 PM			
1:00 PM			

Time	Day 1	Day 2	Day 3
1:30 PM			
2:00 PM			
2:30 PM			
3:00 PM			
3:30 PM			
4:00 PM			
4:30 PM			
5:00 PM			
5:30 PM			
6:00 PM			
6:30 PM			
7:00 PM			
7:30 PM			
8:00 PM			
8:30 PM			
9:00 PM			
9:30 PM			
10:00 PM			
10:30 PM			
11:00 PM			
11:30 PM			
12:00 AM			
12:30 AM			
1:00 AM			
1:30 AM			
2:00 AM			
2:30 AM			
3:00 AM			
3:30 AM			
4:00 AM			
4:30 AM			
5:00 AM			

Step 2: Review your time study: Ask yourself the following questions as you review your time study. Write the answers down.

What am I wasting time on?

Are there any time leaks? Time leaks are tasks where you waste time or lose track of time on non-value added activities. This is an area where everything in moderation is okay. Too much of anything needs to be addressed. Time leaks include:

Too much social media
Too much email
Too much TV
Too many video games
Too much socializing
Misplacing things (spending too much time looking for things)
Forgetting things (spending time running back home or to office to get)

Could I be clustering any activities? Remember, clustering is the act of organizing groups of tasks that have something in common. Examples include: paying bills, returning phone calls, responding to email, running errands around town.

Are there things I can delegate? Delegating is assigning the task to someone else. Review Strategy #2: Ask for help to improve in this area.

Are there things I can say NO to? Review Strategy #3: Learn to say NO to improve in this area.

This time study produces many "ah-ha" moments. It creates an awareness of how much time you actually waste. Once you become aware of how something is negatively affecting your opportunity to **Live Life Beyond The Laundry,** you will increase your probability to successfully make a change. We mindlessly do so many activities during the day we don't realize how much time we waste. I have had people tell me after completing this activity they did not realize they spent ten hours watching TV over the weekend or three hours a night on social media. Just that realization alone made them change their priorities, therefore allowing them to get more done in less time.

Living Life Beyond the Laundry = Balancing Life

Time = life; therefore, waste your time and waste your life, or master your time and master your life. ~Alan Lakein

The key is in not spending time, but in investing it. ~Stephen R. Covey

A Very Bizzy Check In

Hey, it's Bizzy again. I like this strategy…focused balancing act. That describes my life. The old me used to spend all day reacting to what happened next. It was very overwhelming, exhausting and stressful. Now I plan my days and they run so much smoother. The 10-minute Power Plan works; it is my life saver.

I am almost embarrassed to say my co-workers and friends have noticed a change in me. Many people have come up to me in the last couple of weeks and said, "Bizzy, you seem so much happier and less stressed. What are you doing differently?" I then share my new love in life with them…the 10-minute Power Plan.

Unplanned things still pop up during the day, but I react much better to them since it only happens a couple of times a day versus a couple of times an hour. Truly amazing! Reminds me of the power of a positive attitude tool.

Chapter 9

Strategy #5: Stop Procrastinating NOW

*Procrastination is the bad habit of putting off
until the day after tomorrow what should have been done
the day before yesterday. ~Napoleon Hill*

Definition: Procrastination is the act or habit of putting off or delaying something requiring immediate attention.

Let's learn more about procrastination and how you can prevent it from controlling your life. It's time for you to make things happen. It will result in more time for what's really important. Life was meant to be lived, not procrastinated.

There are many forms of procrastination. The key to putting a stop to procrastination is to identify why you procrastinate. I spent several hours reading and researching the topic of procrastination, even though there was laundry to do. But it was me or the dirty underwear, and I decided to put myself first. This research, combined with coaching many people, lead me to create the categories of procrastination below. This not an all-inclusive list; however, it contains the most common reasons why people procrastinate. To gain a clear understanding of procrastination, let's discuss the details of each of the procrastination reasons.

1. Procrastination by Perfectionism

This is one key area I have had to combat. Yes, combat is the correct word here. When you identify why you most often procrastinate, you can create a strategy to move through the wall of procrastination. A few years back, I did not even realize that perfectionism was a form of procrastination; however, it is one of the hardest to combat because we want everything perfect.

This book is a perfect example of procrastination by perfectionism. I have been trying to write *Live Life Beyond the Laundry* for about five years now. I finally figured out that I just needed to get the words out of my head and on paper into a rough draft. It took me five years to realize that a rough draft was an acceptable starting point. I was stuck because I wanted the first draft to be the perfect final product. I was stuck on page ten for five years. Once I realized this, I began to make progress.

People who struggle with procrastination by perfectionism avoid getting out of the gate for fear they won't cross the finish line.

2. Overwhelmed Procrastination (Too many options)

Often people don't know where to start or what to choose. It's a double-edged sword. Having choices is important, but having too many choices causes chaos and confusion. When there are too many choices, people make snap decisions just to get it over with, delegate to someone else, or just do nothing.

This is why when parents teach and communicate to young children, they give them two or three choices. Would you like oatmeal, cereal or toast for breakfast? The kids can easily make a decision from those choices.

Adults are really not that far from the above story. We think we want 20 choices; however, we get frustrated when given so many choices. We actually prefer three or four choices. Think of the last time you purchased a computer, kitchen appliance or bed. There were so many choices that you were unable to compare apples to apples. You became frustrated and possibly did not make the best decision. Did you go home with an end table?

If you are struggling with being overwhelmed as a form of procrastination, narrow down your choices and move forward.

3. Procrastination by Fear of Failure

Even the most confident people fear failing at something so they put off working toward a goal or achievement. If they don't start, they won't fail. Failure is good. This is how we learn life's lessons. Change the word failure to stumbling; we all stumble in life. The difference between successful people and unsuccessful people is that successful people learn from stumbling. They pick themselves up and keep moving forward. Unsuccessful people quit. Which are you?

A good example is public speaking. People fear making a mistake in front of a large crowd because it might make them look like a fool. The audience will not even notice a mistake unless you point it out to them. Push beyond the fear and give it a try.

4. Procrastination by Lack of Knowledge

You lack the knowledge to complete a task or project. You really don't want to take the time or bother someone to ask how to complete the task. You think you should already know how to do this task, so you hesitate to ask for help. This may be something you simply don't enjoy and just don't want to take the time to learn about. Maybe if you just ignore this task it will go away. It won't go away.

5. Procrastination by Distraction

The day is filled with distractions. The following are a few distractions that sometimes prevent people from getting everything they need to do done during the day (email, meetings, dirty dishes, kids, pets, time, household chores, multi-tasking, and interruptions). You can place anything on the list that takes the focus away from the task or project you are working on.

Studies indicate that it takes roughly six minutes to refocus after an interruption has taken your attention away from the activity you were working on. If you eliminate distractions and interruptions, I guarantee you will get more done in less time.

Sometimes we use distractions as an excuse or justification of why we did not get something done. This is the blame game. Learn to focus and you will not need to make excuses.

6. Procrastination by Wrong Goal

Too often, people's ideas about their goals come from outside sources. What friends and family think we SHOULD do with our lives, jobs, and families has a huge influence on us. They are often unhappy with their life outcomes, so they try to influence your life in order to live vicariously through you.

What does living your life to the fullest look like for you? Not knowing this will prevent you from moving forward to successfully achieve your goals and dreams. Figure out what you want in life, not what someone else tells you to want. You are the person who has to do the work and live with the end result.

That is one of the main reasons successful people are unhappy—something is missing in their lives. They are living somebody else's life rather than a life that would make them happy. So are they really successful? They are really just successful in one part of their life and unhappy in many other parts. Living a happy, complete life is also an important puzzle piece to success.

We have all heard stories about people who went to college for a career their parents thought they should pursue. For example, Melissa's parents really wanted her to be a doctor, so she went to medical school for 12 years. She really didn't enjoy being a doctor, but her parents were so proud of her. She really wanted to be an artist, but they did not support her because they didn't think she could be financially stable as an artist.

Whose life is it? Ask yourself...is there anything in your life that fits into the Procrastination by Wrong Goal reason? What do you really want to do? Did the above questions make you think of something that needs changing in your life? Build a strategy and move forward. This is scary because it is change, and people only like change when it does not affect them.

7. Procrastination by Loss of Motivation

When they work to achieve a goal or complete an activity, many people experience a loss of motivation. We think of an idea and go after it with enthusiasm. But before we know it, we lose steam and stop progressing forward. Dealing with emotional highs and lows is an experience common to all people. Typically, we accept our emotions as beyond our control. So we simply quit.

This is called "all or nothing" mentality and is a huge barrier to successfully **Live Life Beyond the Laundry**. For example, you decide you are going to start an exercise routine starting Monday morning.

You do fantastic week one and feel great, you get busy week two with work and the kids and simply do not make time to exercise. You quickly lose motivation. Turn it around, build a strategy and get moving again versus quitting.

Now that you understand the forms of procrastination, I can reassure you that everyone procrastinates from time to time. You will never remove all procrastination from your life, but identifying areas where you let it get away from you will help you take back control. Procrastination quickly takes over and can prevent you from living life to the fullest. Take a look at the questions below. If procrastination has ever resulted in one of the following, you have room for growth in Strategy #5.

- Have you ever lost money as a result of procrastination?
- Have you ever missed a deadline as a result of procrastination?
- Have you ever missed a great opportunity as a result of procrastination?
- Have you ever been stressed as a result of procrastination?
- Have you ever had to defend yourself or justify your actions as a result of procrastination?

If you answered YES to any of the questions above, you can learn to build a strategy to bust through the wall of procrastination. Why lose money or excellent opportunities because you waited too long? We have all been there; learn from your mistakes.

I can answer YES to a few of the above and could just kick myself. For example, last year we signed up for vision insurance, thinking two or three of our family members would need glasses over the course of the year. We had our checkups in January and learned that we did not need glasses other than inexpensive reading glasses. I had an opportunity to cancel the vision insurance and didn't because I wasn't quite sure how to make that happen. A couple of times during the year, I thought about it but never took care of it because I did not know how. So instead of asking how, I just didn't do it. It ended up costing me $250 for the year and I had to think about it multiple times during the year (hello, BMS). If I had just asked for help and learned how to cancel the insurance, I would have been $250 richer. Instead, I chose to procrastinate. That may not seem like much money, but what else could I have done with that money? Here is what $250 will buy:

- 3 luxurious massages ("Me" Time)
- 5 relaxing pedicures ("Me" Time)
- 63 lattés ("Me" Time)
- 1.5 fun nights at a water park hotel (family time)
- 1 romantic night in a suite with a Jacuzzi (date night)

So I guess procrastination resulted in my loss, my family's loss and the loss of a romantic date night. Check, lesson learned. Next time I will ask how to complete the task because I am certain it would have taken me about five minutes to complete if I had just asked.

By the way, this is not the only question I answered YES to (see, even I expect myself to be brutally honest). I was assigned a project at work and had nine months to complete the task. I was asked to write a manual for a new computer program that was going to be introduced. Six months passed and I really had not done anything to complete the manual (if I had only known about Power Planning back then). I kept telling myself and my manager that I was just too busy with all my other work to get to it. I told myself that so much that I actually began to believe it. I was very convincing.

One day I was sitting down with my manager, and he asked me about the manual. He was just checking in to see how it was moving forward since I only had three more months to the deadline. At that point, I had to fess up to the fact that I really only had about 1/10th of the manual done.

What happened next was a turning point in my life. My manager asked me why I was not further, and I explained how busy I had been with my other work. I truly believed that was the reason WHY. My manager helped me break the project down into manageable tasks, gave me milestones to reach and deadlines to meet. At this point, I realized I had been procrastinating.

The reasons why I was procrastinating? Perfectionism, being

overwhelmed, lack of knowledge and not asking for help.

Needless to say, as a result of that meeting, I produced a great training manual. Here are the steps in the strategy I created:

- Create an outline.
- Create milestone goals versus just looking at the big picture (100 pages).
- Complete a brain dump and just put the information down on paper (perfection not necessary).
- Then go back and fill in more detail.

When you admit that procrastination negatively affects your life, you can figure out why you're doing it. Then you can build a strategy to move forward. You can bust through the wall of procrastination. I did not think I was a procrastinator until I began researching and reading about it. As soon as I admitted that I do procrastinate, I began to **Live Life Beyond the Laundry.** It created the awareness I needed to move forward to achieve results and success.

Procrastination Strategy Tool

The purpose of this tool is to help you gain a clear understanding of what you are procrastinating, the reason for procrastinating, and how to build a strategy to bust through the wall of procrastination.

Step 1: Gain a clear understanding of why people procrastinate by reading about the above reasons.

Step 2: Admit that you procrastinate from time to time.

Step 3: Using the space below, make a list of five items you are currently procrastinating about in your life. This can be as small as cleaning out the hall closet and as big as going back to school.

Step 4: Using the space provided, write down the reason you are procrastinating. Using the seven categories above, maybe there's more than one category.

Step 5: Using the space provided, develop a strategy to overcome procrastinating each of your five items. The next section has ideas to help.

Step 6: Put the strategies into action. Power Plan them into your day.

Step 7: Celebrate your success.

Use the following form to complete the above steps.

Procrastination #1: _____

Reason Why: _____

Strategy to overcome procrastination:_____

_____

Procrastination #2: _____

Reason Why: _____

Strategy to overcome procrastination:_____

_____

Procrastination #3: _____

Reason Why: _____

Strategy to overcome procrastination:_____

_____

Procrastination #4: _____

Reason Why: _____

Strategy to overcome procrastination:_____

_____

Procrastination #5: _____

Reason Why: _____

Strategy to overcome procrastination:_____

_____

Sample strategies to shift beyond procrastination:

1. Select a mantra or a slogan to remind yourself to move
    forward when you begin to feel like you are stalling out.
    There are several I use during a week. Feel free to use
    one of mine or create your own, as long as it inspires and
    motivates you.
    • Daily action creates results. I say this multiple times a
      day to myself and to my coaching clients.
    • It is never too late to start the day over. I have this
      posted in my kitchen as a visual reminder when I am
      having a challenging day.
    • Internal success + External success = Balancing. I have
      this posted on my vision board as a reminder.
    • Progress, not perfection.
    • Slow down to move faster.
    • *Blessed are the flexible for they shall not be bent out of
      shape.* ~author unknown.

2. Divide and conquer. Break the task down into manageable tasks. It will not seem as overwhelming, and then just do the next most important task to move the goal or activity forward. Think of it this way. How do you eat an elephant? One bite at a time.

3. As Brian Tracy says, "Eat that frog." Do what you have been procrastinating first thing in the morning and just get it over with. Then you don't have to spend the day, week or even month thinking about it.

4. Delegate. You may not be the right person to complete the task. What you find unpleasant, someone else might actually enjoy.

5. Focus and eliminate distractions. A tool I use daily is a kitchen timer. I need to pick my child up at school every day at 2:30 so, at about 1:00 each day I set a timer so I can focus on completing my work without looking at the clock. I know the timer will remind me when it is time to go. The kitchen timer provides focus to complete any activity when you have another time-related event at some point during the day.

6. Ride the momentum. Once you get going, keep going. Time-blocking an afternoon or day for a big project helps with this strategy.

7. Clarify your goals to make them clear and concise.

8. Research the form of procrastination you identify as your most challenging on the Internet. This is what I did with perfectionism, and the information I learned was instrumental in moving me forward to success.

9. Hire a life coach.

10. Implement the strategies and tools in **Live Life Beyond the Laundry.**

When you identify why you're procrastinating something and develop a strategy to propel you forward, you greatly increase your ability to **Live Life Beyond the Laundry.**

Living Life Beyond the Laundry = Balancing Life

*The key is not to prioritize what's on your schedule,
but to schedule your priorities.* ~Stephen Covey

*Know the true value of time; snatch, seize, and enjoy every moment
of it. No idleness, no laziness, no procrastination: never put off till
tomorrow what you can do today.* ~Lord Chesterfield

A Very Bizzy Check In

Hey, it's Bizzy again. At first I did not like this strategy. I thought, I never procrastinate. I just check it off and get it done. I am so busy, how I can possibly be procrastinating?

Well, I was sadly mistaken here. As I learned about the reasons why people procrastinate, I kept thinking of examples in my life. I was actually quite appalled by my findings.

Needless to say, I worked the Procrastination Strategy Tool and created strategies to complete what I had been procrastinating. I feel so much better about what I have been able to accomplish. This is a tool I keep using over and over. It really helps to get things done when I have a strategy to make it happen.

One of the items I was procrastinating was my closet. It was a disaster. I built a strategy to organize it, and now it looks great. It only took me an hour to complete the task. I can now find anything I need right away. Sometimes I walk back to my closet just to see how great it looks. I love how that makes me feel.

Chapter 10

Strategy #6 Busy Mind Syndrome

The best cure for insomnia is to get a lot of sleep. ~ *W. C. Fields*

Definition: Busy Mind Syndrome, otherwise known as BMS, is the inability to turn your brain off at night or to stay focused during the day. An example is, as you try to sleep, you replay the day over and over or think about everything you need to do.

Busy mind syndrome makes is difficult to sleep and focus on your daily schedule and responsibilities. This strategy focuses on understanding the root causes of BMS and how to use tools to reduce it. Some of the common causes of BMS are mommy guilt, over-committed schedules, unrealistic expectations we create for ourselves, and the never ending to-do list. Let's face it. Who doesn't want a little less BMS in their lives?

Marcus Aurelius said, "A man's life is what his thoughts make of it." As you go sleep at night, your mind races through all kinds of stuff in your head. This includes all your thoughts, ideas, chores, appointments, commitments, relationships, conversations, and events (past and future). This is called BMS, or brain clutter. BMS prevents us from getting the six-eight hours of quality sleep required for an adult to function effectively and productively throughout the day.

BMS creates stress and chaos in our brains. Think of a spot in your house that is very unorganized and cluttered. What feelings surface as you think of this spot? Stress? Chaos? Do you feel overwhelmed with the thought of tackling it? Your body reacts the same way when your brain has clutter.

Have you ever:
- Awakened up four to six times during the night thinking about what you have to do the next day?
- Placed something unusual in the refrigerator, like your cell phone?
- Gone to work with two different shoes on?
- Looked at the concert tickets for tonight and realized the concert was two days ago?
- Dialed a phone number and forgot who you were calling?
- Been driving down the road and forgot where you were going?

Let's talk about each of the common causes and learn tools to reduce BMS.

Mommy Guilt

Many people I visit with express feeling guilty weekly, if not daily. They jokingly say, "Oh, I am a Catholic. I have to feel guilty." That is their attempt to justify this feeling of guilt. It's the one accessory no mother is ever without. You become conditioned to think that you should be able to do everything because you're the mom. If you can't do everything, there must something wrong with you.

Guilt is that feeling that zaps your precious energy, a commodity we are already deficient in. "When guilt starts to take the enjoyment out of your day-to-day life with kids, that's when you know it's time to address it," says Devra Renner, a mom of two and co-author of the book *Mommy Guilt*. Below are some common causes of mommy guilt:

- Working.
- I don't spend enough time with my kids.
- I yelled at my kids.
- I don't invite their friends over enough.
- I want to do something with my friends.
- I bought my kids generic clothes versus name brand.

The list is endless. What does yours look like?

Part of striving for work/life balance is reducing mommy guilt. Did you know your kids will enjoy the time you spend with them more when they don't sense your mommy guilt? Kids are smart; they sense when you're spending time with them purely because you feel guilty. It is an unrealistic expectation to eliminate all mommy guilt. However, strive to reduce it, and embrace the fact you'll have a little bit no matter how far beyond the laundry you live your life.

Over-committed Schedules

This includes your schedule, your family schedule, and your children's schedule. Do you have too much going on? Every minute of the day does not need to be scheduled. Just kick back and enjoy life.

It's one thing to be tired or worn-out from time to time. It happens to all of us. But it's another to be tired and worn-out all the time. This not only keeps you from being the loving parent, wife, sister, friend you are or want to be, but also presents a threat to your health and your ability to strive for work/life balance.

It's time to clean up your schedule. The Purge the Schedule tool below, along with reviewing Strategy # 3, learning to say NO, will help with an over-committed schedule.

Unrealistic Expectations and the Never-ending to-do List

Busy women tend to create unrealistic expectations for themselves each day. Remember: there are only 24 hours in a day and only so much can be accomplished in a 24-hour period. First and foremost is six-eight hours of sleep. Sleep plays an instrumental role in striving for work/life balance. When we give ourselves permission to sleep six-eight hours each night, we're more productive and energized for the remaining hours of the day. You'll get more done in less time.

Learn to set yourself up for success versus failure each day by creating realistic expectations. Do you really think you can get all 20 items on your list completed today? If the answer is YES because they are fairly quick tasks, that is a realistic expectation. If the answer is NO, only write down what you need to get done today. Place the other items further out in your calendar. Give yourself permission to set realistic expectations for yourself each and every day. This leaves time for family, friends, "Me" Time, and simply enjoying life to the fullest.

Funny Story:

Have you ever been so excited that you were caught up on the laundry that you stood in the laundry room and took off the clothes you were wearing to put them in the last load of laundry just so you could say, "Yay, every piece of laundry is done"? Then you do a little naked happy dance in the laundry room because the laundry is all done. Many women secretly do this and, if you are not one of them, you may just start.

So let's dig into the tools to help move you forward to reduce

BMS in your life. Once you put them into action, I guarantee you'll reduce brain clutter. This will allow you to sleep better at night and focus better during the day.

Purge the Schedule Tool

The purpose of this tool is to clean up your schedule. Just like cleaning out the refrigerator, it needs to be done from time to time.

Step 1: Look at your schedule for the next month. Review every activity/meeting/commitment and ask yourself the following questions. You started this in Strategy #3, but you might have missed something. This activity will help you identify more commitments to eliminate. Write the activities you find; then answer the following questions.

- Why am I doing this activity?
- Do I enjoy this activity?
- Do I enjoy the people there?
- What is my motivation for why I feel committed to this activity?
- Who will be most disappointed if I cancel/quit/put on permanent hold?
- Do I care?
- When can I end this obligation?
- What next action can I take to change my obligation? It may be quitting, or just scaling back.

Step 2: Ask your children the above questions about their schedules and write what you learn below. Do they need to be in a sport, music lesson, Girl Scouts, and speech team all at the same time? Sometimes the answer might be YES. One thing I have noticed with my kids is that they enjoy the down weeks between sports seasons when we can just stay home. This observation has resulted in discussions with my children to sign up only for what they truly enjoy.

Step 3: Keep doing what you enjoy and build a strategy to remove what you don't enjoy. This allows more time for what's really important, allowing you to **Live Life Beyond the Laundry**.

Reframe It Tool

This tool is to help busy working women learn to reframe self-talk to feel inspired and motivated rather than defeated and stressed by their day.

Step 1: Ask yourself the following questions and write down your answers explaining why, not just YES and NO.

- Do your ever feel that what you do just isn't good enough?
- Do you ever feel like a failure?
- Do you ever feel regret or guilt because you should have done something differently?

Step 2: If you answered YES to any of the above, you sometimes hold yourself to unrealistic standards. Reframe what you say to yourself, and you will end your day with a feeling of inspiration versus defeat. Below are examples of reframing what you say to yourself.

What we say: If I'd only done _____ instead.
Reframe it: Next time I will do this _____ instead. We learn from our lessons in life.

What we say: Looking back, I should have done _____
Reframe it: At the time I did my best. Next time I will_____

What we say: I am too busy to do _____
Reframe it: I am too busy not to schedule time to _____

What we say: I did not accomplish anything today.
Reframe it: I did my best. Now I can rest. I am confident that I am a success. Give it a try.

Reframing
what you think and say out loud significantly increases happiness, positive thoughts and enables you to **Live Life Beyond the Laundry**.

What Are You Tolerating Tool

The purpose of this tool is to reduce BMS and brain clutter by completing a brain dump. We all have things in our lives we tolerate, procrastinate and put up with. Many of these things detract from our ability to **Live Life Beyond the Laundry**. They reduce the quality and satisfaction of our lives. Numerous studies indicate that creating a toleration list is a useful tool to reduce the stress and chaos created by brain clutter. By simply listing the things we don't want, we begin the process of their removal or completion.

Step 1: Set aside 20 minutes of uninterrupted time.

Step 2: Take out a piece of paper or use a page at the end of this book.

Step 3: List everything you tolerate in your life. Don't analyze, just list. What in your life are you putting up with, settling for, or procrastinating? This is more than a to-do list. It's a to-do list on steroids. After 15 minutes, you may run out of ideas. Keep sitting there and thinking. On minute 18, you may come up with the best idea of what you are tolerating.

Examples may include:
- Leaky faucet. You give little thought to it; however, it bothers you every time you enter the kitchen.
- Painting the upstairs, updating your resume, organizing baby pictures, planting a garden, hockey fund-raising committee, school carnival committee.

Step 4: You have completed your brain dump. The clutter is out of your head and on a piece of paper.

Step 5: Post this on the side of your refrigerator. One reason for brain clutter is that we are worried we'll forget something. Now that it's on paper, you won't forget it. You are what you think about so, if your brain is always busy, even when you sleep, that is what you are creating for yourself.

BMS Elimination (mini-tools)

The purpose of this tool is to provide tips to help you sleep better and reduce BMS. BMS is a huge energy drain, so work to eliminate it.

***Mini Tool:** Routine sleep hours. Go to sleep and wake up at the same time every day, even on weekends. Think of it this way: If you wake up at 6:00 on the weekends and your kids wake up at 8:00, that's two hours to do whatever you want to do. You will love this "Me" Time.

***Mini Tool:** Keep a notepad and pen by your bed. If you wake up in the middle of the night, write your thoughts down. No need to turn on the light; just the act of writing it down will help you sleep better. You won't forget about it because you've written it down. You'll also get a laugh in the morning looking at your midnight scribbles.

***Mini Tool:** Keep a gratitude journal. Each night before you go to bed, write down five things you're grateful for. It will help you realize all that is great in your life.

****Mini Tool:** Remember the toleration list you created above? Have a toleration party. Have your best friend complete a toleration list. Designate two Sundays in a row to have a toleration party. One day you go to her house. She provides the chocolate and margaritas! Plow through a chunk of her toleration list. The next Sunday, she comes to your house and you provide the chocolate and margaritas. As a team, you plow through your toleration list. A toleration party makes it more fun, encourages quality time with a friend, and reduces your stress and chaos.

Give these tools a try or create your own. If you create a great one, send me an email and I will add it to my list. BMS is just about as annoying as PMS. Sometimes you can reduce the symptoms of PMS with tips and tricks you learn from friends. You can reduce the symptoms of BMS the same way. Give it a try and enjoy the results.

It's Not in My Hula-Hoop Tool

The purpose of this tool is to help remove some of the BMS from your life. Part of what causes chaos in some people's lives is the need to fix things, even things they have no business or ability to fix. The urge to make everyone happy and have everything run smoothly is exhausting. The need to make sure everything is fair and equal is overwhelming and can keep people awake at night. This can consume both your personal and professional life. Soon people realize they need to figure out how to step away from things if they aren't able to fix or control them, especially if they can't be fixed or controlled. A tool that helps figure this out is my hula-hoop.

Step 1: Imagine yourself standing inside a hula-hoop. If you really struggle with the need to control a situation or the urge to make everyone happy, actually buy one from the toy store and stand inside it.

Step 2: Evaluate things that come your way and imagine if they are "in your hula-hoop" or not.

Step 3: If they aren't, then move on and leave them to someone else. If they don't affect you or they are things you can't fix or control, then they aren't in your hula-hoop and you should let them go.

Step 4: If they are in your hula-hoop, build a strategy to take care of them and move forward.

Living Life Beyond the Laundry = Balancing Life

The greatest revolution of our generation is the discovery that human beings, by changing the inner attitudes of their minds, can change the outer aspects of their lives. ~William James

A Very Bizzy Check In

Hey, it's Bizzy again. You can just say BIG eye opener here. No wonder I was waking up five times a night and was exhausted all day. My brain was full of clutter. I was experiencing extreme BMS.

I LOVE this strategy. I completed the toleration list and it's up on my refrigerator so I know I won't forget anything. I sleep like a baby all night long. I rarely wake up during the night and I can't believe how great I feel when my alarm goes off in the morning. No more swearing at the alarm clock for me.

It is amazing how much better the morning goes with my kids when I am rested. I don't get frustrated and yell at them before they leave for school. I have eliminated mommy guilt in that area.

I have shared this tool with many of my friends and they are reporting fantastic results. I already knew they had before they told me, because I noticed they looked happier and rested. Ahhhh, success! It feels good to help my friends out.

Chapter 11

Chaos Reduction Strategy #7:
Why Reinvent the Laundry Basket?

It takes as much energy to wish as it does to plan. *~Eleanor Roosevelt*

Definition: Why Reinvent the Laundry Basket is to learn from others. Your family and friends have many great ideas and they will share them if you ask.

This is a special chapter. Many of my friends shared their personal success stories and strategies. Learn from my friends, and then start learning from your friends.

Simply put, we all have tips, strategies and tools we use each day. Share the knowledge. The tools in Strategies #1 through #6 I learned from friends, family, co-workers, and research. I modified many of them 1) to meet the unique needs of my family and 2) based on additional research that made the tools even better.

If you have a tool or strategy that works, share it. This strategy is a compilation of miscellaneous tips and success stories I have learned from others. Like me, if you learn something from a friend, feel free to modify it to meet the unique needs of your family or, even better, share it with someone you see struggling in that area of their life. Just say to your friend, "I just learned about a great tool and it has made such a difference in my life. Would you like to hear about it?"

With this strategy, you will learn an important communication technique about providing feedback. Because providing feedback and sharing stories with others takes skill and practice, it is important that you do not criticize or judge. Reframe it into a positive message; it will be even more effective and will not leave your friend feeling guilty or judged. Reframing a message to positive is a powerful tool.

One tool I have many people share is the Power of a Positive Attitude Tool. They say, "Christy, I have this one negative person who sits by me at work. This would be such a great tool for them." Now you cannot go up to that person and say, "You are very negative. I just learned about this tool that would be very helpful for you." They would be very insulted and hurt. Instead, reframe it and tell your whole work team at the next staff meeting, "I learned about this great new tool and it has been very helpful to me. I thought it would be fun if we all did it together." Huge difference in delivery and results.

If you have a success story or tool to share with me, I would love to hear about it. Email me at Christy@SimplyBalancedCoaching. com and I will add it to my collection. Enjoy the stories.

Having a bad day? Turn it around: Jessica Tryhus

Sometimes you just wake up on the wrong side of the bed. We all have mornings like this. Or you planned to have a good day, but you receive a frustrating email or a co-worker/family member says something that drives you crazy. This completely sends your day into a tailspin. What can you do to turn it around?

Follow this 3-step process to turn it around.
- Make a choice to turn your day around versus just having a terrible day.
- Create a strategy to move your day forward. Think of what the next best step is to move your challenge/obstacle forward, then put it into action.
- Then fake it. Pretend you are having a good day and have a positive attitude. Before you know it, you'll be having a good day with a positive attitude. Your subconscious mind believes what you tell it and works to make it a reality.

I utilized this tip while visiting with a coaching client. She had a very challenging morning. We talked her through the above three steps, and she completely turned her day around. Her day went from terrible to terrific. Fantastic results. So, the next time you are having a difficult day, turn it around.

Sock Solution: Lori Haarstad

Point blank, I hate laundry. Anything I can do to not waste any time in my life doing laundry is key. For instance, what anal retentive person came up with the idea that we are all incompetent if we don't spend hours matching socks? We all know everyone has a pile of mismatched socks somewhere that we are sure their matches will turn up in the next load. Know what? They never do! Everyone knows it, but we keep up the folding-and-matching-socks routine because that is what all "organized" people do. Charade!

Do you have any idea how many hours are wasted by matching those things? The stupid drawer gets messed up anyway when you're looking for a certain pair, especially in the kids' drawers. My answer? Forget it. Each person has a basket of socks in their closet, including me. Toss all your socks in that basket and find a match as needed.

Marketing genius! They now sell mismatched socks together, probably because that person was sick of matching them. I only buy certain kinds of socks for each kid so I know right where they go. The "fun" ones stand out and the kids know which are theirs. Now sock laundry is easy, and I can go do something worth my time. No one will ever know the difference.

Just do it NOW: Stacy Hanson

I really took to heart the advice from "The Happiness Project" that said, "If it takes less than a minute, just do it now." Don't put it off. Instead of letting a dish sit by the dishwasher, just put it inside. If you are looking at an unmade bed, just make it now and don't let it bother you. The minute rule works great for me and I get a LOT more accomplished. Smaller tasks are finished quickly and they don't pile up!

Plan Ahead: Mary Kuehn

Mornings can be busy, chaotic and stressful. I get a jump on this by getting everything organized the night before versus in the morning. I lay out my clothes, pack my lunch and put my school bags back into the car, and I get the coffee ready. I know that I am not a morning person so this is very helpful. The ten minutes I take each night to plan ahead greatly reduces morning stress and helps me sleep better.

Start the Day Out Right: Donna Wheeler

I'm not an evening planner, but my mind loves to start planning the day before I'm even out of bed in the morning. And so my day begins.

I make sure I have a full night's sleep, get up before everyone else, and start the coffee pot. I exercise while I plan my day (power plan on the treadmill). Start with a power breakfast of approximately 30g protein. Then I'm ready to wake the family and start the day! Yes, I love my to-do list, but good sleep, exercise and a protein breakfast are just as valuable to me.

Power Plan: Mindy Christenson

I keep a running inventory of what is in my chest freezer and plan a few days' worth of meals at a time. On the days my kids have me running I make supper in the crock pot while my kids are eating breakfast. I also keep a running grocery list on my refrigerator and write down things when they get low instead of waiting until I'm out.

I try planning my errands (post office, grocery store, bank, etc.) around picking up and dropping off my daughter from school so I don't have to make multiple trips out during the day. This allows me to focus on my work versus being distracted with everything I need to do.

I've discovered I must keep a small notepad with me at all times, including at night on the bedside table, because if I think of something (errands, phone calls), I must write it down or I'll forget.

Insightful Information: Melissa Bell

Organizing is just like eating. Take smaller bites so you can chew and swallow. Don't let it pile up or you won't get anywhere! What great insight!

This past spring I created a 40-day organizing challenge with a group of my friends. Each night, we selected a location in our house to organize and clean. It ranged from a cleaning a kid's closet to organizing the storage room. The fun part was that we cheered each other on and gave each other great ideas for the next night. My house looked great after 40 days. So rewarding and yet relaxing.

Simple Steps: Tami Enfield

I have recently found it helpful to make a list of steps required to move forward on a specific goal. Make sure these items promote a positive feeling for you. Then have someone hold you accountable to this list. Christy Tryhus did a phenomenal job holding me accountable!

Thank you to all my fantastic friends for sharing.

Just Ask Tool

The purpose of this tool is to help you begin learning from others. Why reinvent the laundry basket?

Step 1: List the names of three friends or family members you think successfully **Live Life Beyond the Laundry** in some part of their lives.

Step 2: Power Plan time to call them to ask them how they do it. Better yet, Power Plan a lunch or coffee date with them to enjoy some time together. What did you learn from them? Would that tool work in your life?

Step 3: If you are struggling with something and you notice one of your friends or family members does a great job in this area, ask them how they do it and learn from them. They don't know what you don't know. Why reinvent the laundry basket?

Living Life Beyond the Laundry = Balancing Life

Simplify, let it go, reduce, eliminate, make it work, balance, pamper, live with joy, take time, relax, refocus, live simply, renew, enjoy life, laugh, love, dance, giggle, smile, Simplify. ~source unknown

A Very Bizzy Check In

Hey, it's Elizabeth. Yes, I have transformed into Elizabeth again. My friends no longer have a reason to call me Bizzy. Yes, you heard right. My friends no longer have a reason to call me Bizzy.

Meet the new and improved Elizabeth Tisdale. My friends and family used to have this terrible nickname for me. They called me Bizzy. I have to admit that it really did apply. I was leading a crazy busy life and the nickname fit. I am proud so say I have a new life style. I enjoy life to the fullest!

To set the scene for my life, let's fill in the details: I am married with three kids, one dog, one cat, and four goldfish. We live in a comfortable home, big enough for the five of us. We have a great yard, neighborhood and town. Now I can truthfully say my Christmas card version of life matches my reality.

I have worked through the 7 Strategies to shift my life from chaos to calm and I understand how they work. My life is not always calm and serene; however, I now know what tools to utilize to shift when I am feeling stressed, overwhelmed or chaotic.

I wake up each morning refreshed and ready to put my Power Plan into action. I send my kids off to school with a kiss, a hug, and a happy good-bye versus yelling. I head into work and have a productive day. After work, I head home to enjoy family activities, family time, "Me" Time. I'm fully living life beyond the laundry.

I have learned that life is a journey, and we are always learning and exploring new tools to make life run smoothly.

If I feel myself start to struggle, I go back to the strategies in this book and work through some of the tools again. Again, life is a journey, and you create the results.

A Typical Elizabeth Day

5:45: Alarm goes off

5:49: Roll out of bed and take the dog for a walk. (Oh, it feels so good to be outside listening to the birds chirp and play in the morning.)

6:20: Feed and water the dog.

6:25 Shower time.

6:35: Felt good to take a shower. Coffee time. (I love my coffee.)

6:45: Wake up the kids. (I love waking the kids up.)

6:50: Make breakfast. (It is nice to visit with the kids in the morning. We have extra time for this since everyone got their backpacks and clothes ready the night before for the morning.)

7:05: Kids, time for everyone to get ready for work and school.

7:06: Back to my room to get ready for work.

7:20: Finish getting ready. The bus will be here in four minutes.

7:23: Have a great day at school!

7:28: Put the breakfast dishes in the dishwasher.

7:30: Take dog outside before I head out the door.

7:40: On the road to work.

7:55: And the work day has begun. (I am in a
    productive mood today.)

8:00: Work on project.

9:00: Meeting.

10:00: Meeting.

11:00: Catch up on email.

12:00: Lunch hour. We have a busy night so
    I am going to toss supper in the crock pot when
    I go home for lunch. (I look forward to going
    out to lunch with Ann tomorrow.)

And my day continues in a calm productive fashion.

Chapter 12

It's Possible to Live Life Beyond the Laundry

In order to succeed, your desire for success should be greater than your fear of failure. ~Bill Cosby

Congratulations. What a great start to your journey to **Live Life Beyond the Laundry**. You have done great work on the 7 Strategies to shift life from chaos to calm. What have you learned?

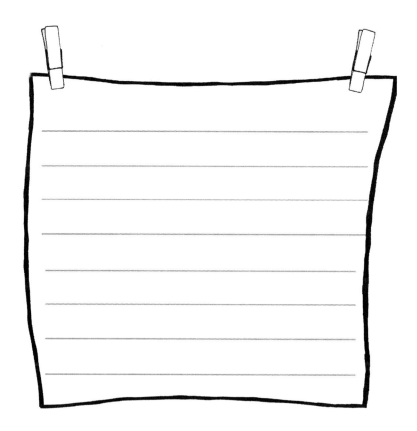

Now it's time to sustain the results you have created. Remember, to **Live Life Beyond the Laundry** takes daily work. When you use the tools in this book, the daily work is much easier. Basically, you have created new habits and this is how you live now.

Life is a journey that may not always move forward. Think of it like going on a hike. There are hills and valleys filled with boulders and ponds. On a hike, these things create the beauty and enjoyment of the hike. Think of life as a hike; daily steps keep you on the journey. You can choose to make the boulder and pond obstacles or you can just go around them and continue on your journey. Life's about choices; make yours.

When you first met Elizabeth, she was living a stressful, busy life. She was consumed with guilt, worry and chaos. She was not really enjoying her kids, job or significant other. She wanted to make some changes and live life to the fullest but did not know where to begin. She realized she had hit a point of extreme chaos and was completely over-whelmed. So she decided to make some changes. She did the work and she now lives life beyond the laundry.

Elizabeth worked hard to incorporate the 7 Strategies to shift life from chaos to calm into her daily life. She made a few modifications along the way to meet the needs of her family. She has made great strides and continues to utilize the tools to create success in her life. Elizabeth is happy, confident and enjoying life to the fullest.

Now it is your turn. Sustain the results of your hard work. If you slip up a bit, that's fine. Just go back to the strategies and tools to figure out what tool you need to move forward again. Remember to continue celebrating your success!

Share everything you have learned with your friends and start a book study group. I have included questions at the back of the book to help guide your book study group to create success. I am available to Skype with your book club for one of your meetings. When you talk about the 7 Strategies and tools with people, you will deepen your level of success.

Keep learning more tools to **Live Life Beyond the Laundry**, follow me on Facebook (Simply Balanced Coaching), Twitter, and at www.LiveLifeBeyond.com. As I create new tools they will be posted on my Blog. Share your success with me; I love to hear success stories from busy working women. Enjoy your journey and remember: daily action creates results!

Success is dependent on effort. ~Sophocles

Live Life Happily Ever After…Beyond the Laundry

Book Club Questions

Chapter 1

- What emotions and thoughts did you experience as you learned about Bizzy Tisdale?
- Did you see a little of your life in Bizzy's story? Explain.
- Are you ready to make some changes in your life? Explain.

Chapter 2

- Do you typically resist change or embrace change?
- Why don't people like change?
- Think back to a significant change in your life. Were you successful? Why or why not?
- Share your vision board with the group.

Chapter 3

- Why do people make excuses?
- What do you think is the most common excuse of busy working women? Explain.
- As you read through the list of excuses, which did you identify as your favorite excuse?
- What is the difference between people who push through obstacles and challenges and the people who give up and let the excuses take control?
- Do you think you have the ability to push beyond the excuses? Explain.

Chapter 4

- What did you learn from Tool #1?
- Do you see the benefit of accepting the challenge in Tool #2?
- Why is it so important to be positive?
- What effect does negativity have on a person?
- Are you ready to make some changes in your life? Explain.

Chapter 5

- How difficult was it to create your "Me" Time menu?
- How difficult was it to take ten minutes each day for "Me" Time?
- How did you feel when you took "Me" Time? (energized, happy, guilty) Share a story with the group.
- Do you see the benefit of taking "Me" Time each day?
- What life skills are you teaching your children by taking "Me" Time?

Chapter 6

- Why is it so difficult for people to ask for help?
- What did you learn about mommy guilt?
- What did you learn from the problem – solution – success tool?
- What are some other ways you can apply the problem – solution – success tool to situations in your life?
- How did the divide-and-conquer activity work for your family?
- Are you ready to make some changes in your life? Explain.

Chapter 7

- Why do you always say YES when you are asked to volunteer, even if you don't really want to do the activity?
- Think of a time when you said YES to an event or activity you wanted to say NO to. Share the story with the group. What did you learn?
- Share one of your exit strategies to remove a SHOULD do activity from your list.
- Are you ready to make some changes in your life? Explain.

Chapter 8

- Why is it important to manage your time wisely?
- How good are you at time management? Explain or share story.
- Share an area you need to improve on regarding time management.
- Which time management tool are you going to incorporate into your life in the next 30 days?

Chapter 9

- Why is procrastination the thief of time?
- What is the reason you typically procrastinate? Explain or share a story.
- Share something you are currently procrastinating. What is your strategy to move it forward?
- Do you have a mantra or slogan? Share it.

Chapter 10

- What do you think about at night when you should be sleeping?
- As you completed your toleration list, what emotions were you experiencing?
- Share something you are currently tolerating. What is your strategy to move it forward?

Chapter 11

- Share one of the stories you learned from someone with your group.
- Why is it so important to learn from others?
- After listening to the stories your book study group shared, share one of the tools you liked and explain how this would help you in your life.

Chapter 12

- What have you done to celebrate your success as you have worked through the strategies and tools?
- What are your next steps to **Live Life Beyond the Laundry**?
- Email me one of your success stories, I would love to learn from you! Christy@SimplyBalancedCoaching.com

About the Author

Christy Tryhus is a certified life coach, author, certified master trainer and college professor. Her business, Simply Balanced Coaching and Training, provides coaching and training to groups, businesses and individuals. She has more than 19 years of experience in training, coaching and sales. This, paired with her passion to help people grow and develop to reach their fullest potential, creates a highly effective training and coaching style.

She received her Master's degree in Business Administration (MBA) at the University of St. Thomas and her Bachelor's degree in Marketing at the University of Wisconsin-Lacrosse.

She has incorporated the 7 strategies in this book into her life over the past ten years. Simply Balanced Coaching and Training specializes in helping busy working women learn to balance all life's responsibilities so they have more time and energy for what's really important.

Christy has a passion for presenting to groups whose busy participants want to learn how shift life from chaos to calm. Her interactive presentation style is valuable to any group size, and she welcomes your inquiries. She also welcomes inquires to Skype with your book Club.

Simply Balanced Coaching & Training
Christy Tryhus
Christy@SimplyBalancedCoaching.com
www.SimplyBalancedCoaching.com

Notes:

Notes:

Time Study Tool

Time	Day 4	Day 5	Day 6
5:30 AM			
6:00 AM			
6:30 AM			
7:00 AM			
7:30 AM			
8:00 AM			
8:30 AM			
9:00 AM			
9:30 AM			
10:00 AM			
10:30 AM			
11:00 AM			
11:30 AM			
12:00 PM			
12:30 PM			
1:00 PM			
1:30 PM			
2:00 PM			
2:30 PM			
3:00 PM			
3:30 PM			
4:00 PM			
4:30 PM			
5:00 PM			
5:30 PM			
6:00 PM			
6:30 PM			
7:00 PM			
7:30 PM			
8:00 PM			
8:30 PM			

Time	Day 4	Day 5	Day 6
9:00 PM			
9:30 PM			
10:00 PM			
10:30 PM			
11:00 PM			
11:30 PM			
12:00 AM			
12:30 AM			
1:00 AM			
1:30 AM			
2:00 AM			
2:30 AM			
3:00 AM			
3:30 AM			
4:00 AM			
4:30 AM			
5:00 AM			

Notes:

_____

_____

_____

_____

_____

_____

_____

_____

_____

Time Study Tool

Time	Day 7	Day 8	Day 9
5:30 AM			
6:00 AM			
6:30 AM			
7:00 AM			
7:30 AM			
8:00 AM			
8:30 AM			
9:00 AM			
9:30 AM			
10:00 AM			
10:30 AM			
11:00 AM			
11:30 AM			
12:00 PM			
12:30 PM			
1:00 PM			
1:30 PM			
2:00 PM			
2:30 PM			
3:00 PM			
3:30 PM			
4:00 PM			
4:30 PM			
5:00 PM			
5:30 PM			
6:00 PM			
6:30 PM			
7:00 PM			
7:30 PM			
8:00 PM			
8:30 PM			

Time	Day 7	Day 8	Day 9
9:00 PM			
9:30 PM			
10:00 PM			
10:30 PM			
11:00 PM			
11:30 PM			
12:00 AM			
12:30 AM			
1:00 AM			
1:30 AM			
2:00 AM			
2:30 AM			
3:00 AM			
3:30 AM			
4:00 AM			
4:30 AM			
5:00 AM			

Notes:

_____

_____

_____

_____

_____

_____

_____

_____

_____

CPSIA information can be obtained at www.ICGtesting.com
Printed in the USA
BVOW010426140512

289983BV00004B/4/P